Burns and Oates

**From the Crib to the Cross**

Meditations for the young

Burns and Oates

**From the Crib to the Cross**
*Meditations for the young*

ISBN/EAN: 9783741197659

Manufactured in Europe, USA, Canada, Australia, Japa

Cover: Foto ©Lupo / pixelio.de

Manufactured and distributed by brebook publishing software (www.brebook.com)

Burns and Oates

**From the Crib to the Cross**

# FROM THE CRIB TO THE CROSS.

The French Edition of this Book,

"DE LA CRÈCHE AU CALVAIRE,"

IS PUBLISHED BY

MESSIEURS POUSSIELQUE FRÈRES,

RUE CASSETTE 15,

PARIS.

*Price 3 Francs.*

# FROM THE CRIB TO THE CROSS.

## MEDITATIONS FOR THE YOUNG;

WITH A PREFACE BY
THE VERY REV. FATHER PURBRICK, PROVINCIAL S.J.

TRANSLATED, WITH THE AUTHOR'S PERMISSION, FROM THE FRENCH OF
"DE LA CRÈCHE AU CALVAIRE,"

---

BURNS AND OATES,
LONDON: | NEW YORK:
GRANVILLE MANSIONS | CATHOLIC PUBLICATION SOCIETY CO.
ORCHARD STREET, W. | BARCLAY STREET.
DUBLIN: M. H. GILL & SONS.

**Nihil obstat.**

A. FAWKES, CONG. ORAT.,
*Censor deputatus.*

**Imprimatur.**

HENRICUS EDUARDUS,
CARD. ARCHIEP. WESTMON.

Die 19 Aprilis, 1884.

## PREFACE.

THERE are many ways of bringing children to Jesus. All are blessed. Those not least which draw them into closest intimacy with Him, and help to make them His true followers and companions.

No one denies that the young can love Him well, and as love implies knowledge, no one ought to deny that they can know Him well, and attain that knowledge by thoughtful study of Him, His ways, His character and His life. Meditation is a hard word, and implies generally the power of following out trains of reasoning, a power not ordinarily possessed in early years. Meditations properly so called, are beyond the reach of most children. But the very young can look and observe; they can watch a person's actions and follow a simple narrative of his life, especially if truthfully and vividly set before their eyes. Where the heart is pure, and the imagination unsullied, the quick wit of childhood, raised and helped by grace, is easily interested in such a Person and life as that of Jesus, and gazing on Him attentively and lovingly, thinks easy thoughts but deep about Him, treasures up each scene in His life, from the Crib of Bethlehem to the Cross of Calvary, and is drawn to the desire of being like Him and copying His ways and conduct. This is contemplation in the Ignatian sense—an easy process, quite as well suited to the young as to the grown up.

Such I take to be the mind of the translator of this little book, in which a pious soul presents in succession the various scenes of our Lord's life, vividly, simply, briefly, so as to arrest the attention of the young, and fix their eyes upon Jesus as a babe, a boy, a man, a victim—as He lives, acts, works and suffers for us—and suggests just those natural, easy, pious thoughts and reflections of which a young mind quickened by grace is capable. No such book has yet appeared in English, and the translator has conceived the happy design of bringing English children in this way to Jesus.

All is simple — language, picture-drawing, study, resolve and prayer. All is true—for it is the Jesus of the Gospels Who is set forth before the young mind. All is practical—for the very words and actions of Jesus are the sole model and examplar which those who use this book are invited to study and reproduce in their own conversation and life.

May He Who so loves and caresses the young,

Whose delight it is to converse with the simple, speak lovingly and inwardly to the multitude of young souls who, as one may hope, will use this book in the way it is intended to be used—daily, thoughtfully, prayerfully!

E. I. PURBRICK, S.J.

*Dec. 16, 1883.*

# INTRODUCTION TO THE FRENCH EDITION.

THE unpretending, pious little work, "*De la Crèche au Calvaire*," was not originally intended for publication. It was the offspring of the author's affection for a child who had just made her First Communion, and was written to serve as a first meditation book for her.

High ecclesiastical advice and pressing demands alone made the author consent to allow his work, but not himself, to be made public. No change was, however, made in the original, simple and even personal arrangement of the book. A devout soul speaks lovingly to another so as to inspire her with a taste for piety.

It is precisely this, that constitutes the most remarkable feature of this little work. In books of meditation the subjects are generally arranged either in too dry a manner, or else they are handled as in a treatise or sermon, so that there is little for the beginner to do, beyond simply perusing each chapter.

Our author has, however, rightly understood that meditation, properly performed, is most useful, if not necessary to, and yet within the reach of, every

# INTRODUCTION TO THE FRENCH EDITION

In presenting this little work, "..." ... ...
..... was not originally intended for publication
..... .. memory of the author's affection for a niece
who ... made her First Communion, and was
written ..... as first meditation book for her.

It ..... advice and pressing ..........
.... ... ..... consent to allow his work, ...
no ..... .. .... ...... No change was ...
.. ... .. ..... ...... and even portion
..... ... .. ........ own speech...

Christian. Indeed the essential acts of a Christian life,—daily prayer, hearing Mass, and frequenting the Sacraments—almost necessarily imply a certain amount of mental prayer. For what else, in fact, but mental prayer, is reflecting a little upon what one says in vocal prayer, uniting one's heart in spirit to the Holy Sacrifice, making interior acts of contrition at Confession, or spending a few minutes in thanksgiving after Holy Communion. The duties of religion appear difficult and hard to many, simply because they fulfil them without entering into their spirit.

But when should initiation into the interior life,—the spiritual religion of the Fathers—begin? Why not at once, before the sweet and holy emotions of First Communion have given place to the preoccupation of pleasures, study or the serious business of life, while the heart is more open to receive the impressions of grace? The way to form true Christians, is to accustom children early, and almost without their knowing it— aye from the very time of their First Communion—to the simple and easy practice of interior converse with God.

The easiest subject of contemplation, alike for the learned and the simple, for the novice and those more advanced in virtue, is the Life of our Lord, with all its wonderful mysteries and various scenes, which, even a child, with its early developed faculties of the memory, the imagination and the heart, has no difficulty in picturing to itself. It is therefore from Jesus' Life on earth that the author has taken all his subjects of meditation. Though thoroughly imbued with St. Ignatius' doctrine, he has rightly thought fit to simplify the plan of the Exercises, so as to retain the same method, without revealing it beforehand. The result of this is that this little book comes nearer to the type of St. Bonaventure's more elementary meditations: but, at the same time, the hand of St. Ignatius is everywhere manifest, and even in places, passages are taken direct from him, as the Preparatory Prayer, for instance, of the sixty third meditation.

Not to overtax the child's attention, the preludes, with the exception of the composition of place, are generally inserted in the Preparatory Prayer, which is always simple and clear, and likely to induce recollectedness. Take, for instance, that before the meditation on the Presentation—" Fill my soul, O my God, with Thy holy Grace, so that I may understand the gift of Himself, which Jesus makes Thee, and endeavour to imitate it:" or that before the meditation on the Arrival of the Holy Family in Egypt:—"Dear Saviour, permit me to remain at Thy Feet, in the presence of Mary and Joseph, and deign to speak to me Thyself."

The composition of place, which, without being

previously spoken of, comes in the exposition of the subject in the first consideration, gives a simple picture on which a child's mind has no difficulty in dwelling, and thus the very imagination is made a help to recollectedness. Many of these descriptions are worthy of note. The author, like St. Ignatius, has developed his first meditation very fully, for the sake of beginners, it is therefore better to take some examples elsewhere, as for instance, when Jesus is first represented sitting by the side of Jacob's Well: "O Lord, let me contemplate and adore Thee. Thou appearest to be alone, but angels surround Thee invisibly, heaven looks upon Thee, and even I am present kneeling at Thy Feet. O divine weariness! It is for me, my Saviour, that Thou sufferest thus. Thy brow is covered with sweat, Thy limbs are bruised with fatigue, and all this to save my soul!" Or again when the Ruler, to whom Jesus has announced that his son is cured, starts homewards: "His faith is not yet sufficiently strong to repel certain anxious workings of his reason. Is his son really cured? Jesus may be deceived. How sad will his return be, if his beloved son should be dead! While he is a prey to these sorrowful reflections, he calculates how many hours it is, since he left his child. Thus the unfortunate father proceeds homewards, more and more overcome by his terrible apprehensions."

The considerations, too, are simple and full of life, and though arranged to conceal their method, follow the plan that, St. Ignatius says, is necessary for the avoidance of distraction and the enjoyment of interior intercourse with God. One seems to see and hear the people represented, and even to take part in what is going on.

The practical applications are such as are most suited to the needs and faults of childhood, and being judiciously arranged, they do not fatigue the mind, nor yet detract from the grandeur of the subject. Thus in the sixty sixth Meditation, the Apostles, wishing to get rid of the crowd that have waited to hear our Lord, and have followed Him right into the desert till evening, say to Him: "Send them away;" and the author, speaking of this indiscretion on the Apostles' part, goes on to remind children of the respect they owe their superiors. Elsewhere Jesus, Who, as the Gospel tells us, "advanced in wisdom and age," is represented at Nazareth as learning St. Joseph's trade as an ordinary apprentice, and is thus addressed: "Dear Jesus, tell me why Thou, Who knowest all things, dost choose to appear ignorant of everything? . . . . . Why not succeed at the first attempt? I seem to hear Thee reply: It is for thee, my child, that I act thus, to teach thee how to work, and to take trouble."

Could a very ordinary and dry lesson be put in a better or more practical way?

The reflections of a meditation book, without being numerous, should be such as may readily serve as examples, and help to suggest others of a similar kind, with which to still further enrich each subject of meditation. And herein the author has succeeded admirably. He puts the child in the way of simple suppositions which seem to arise most naturally, and bring the intended lesson right home to its understanding. Thus, when Jesus was lost at Jerusalem, Mary and Joseph are represented as meeting, in answer to their inquiries, with humiliating replies, and wounding observations about their negligence. And so one is taught to bear reproaches, even when they seem unjust.

The allegorical meaning of the Scriptures is one of the sweetest sources of piety, and in this book the child learns to make use of it. For instance, when numbers of sick persons are brought to Jesus to be cured, and He heals them, the display of charitable zeal makes us understand the necessity of praying for sinners, who are spiritually sick.

One must *carry them to Jesus*, even without their asking it, and sometimes, too, against their will. When they are too heavy for one, then several should unite to carry them, that is, pray for them.

We could cite many other passages, but our object

is merely to make the book known, not to analyse it. It must be used, however, as an instrument of meditation, not simply read. It does not do away with the necessity of personal effort, but encourages and facilitates the practice of it.

We will now let the author speak. We wish his work success. If our humble recommendation could smooth away the difficulties of its first appearance, we should think that we had done something for the glory of God, in helping to extend the salutary practice of mental prayer amongst the young. All Christians deplore the dreadful attacks made on the Church, but perhaps hardly sufficient thought is given to the harm that arises from the indifference, tepidity and want of virtue of her children. In this practical century Religion is judged, not by her doctrines, but by her fruits. The doctrines of our enemies bear fruits of egotism, corruption and hatred. Ah, if all Christians would only show an opposite example; if their lives were different from those of unbelievers; if the dignity of their character, the purity of their morals, their resistance of evil, their zeal for work, and devoted charity, should once more become the distinguishing marks of all who invoke the Name of Jesus Christ, men would be disabused of their errors, and turning again towards the Sign of our Redemption, once more learn from the Gospel the secret of regeneration. But where are the true Christians who cause their religion to be blessed, and not blasphemed? Alas! they are rare in the world. And why? Because the greater number of Catholics have only a surface religion, without any substance, and entirely devoid of the two great pillars of a supernatural life,—prayer and sacrifice. With Christians leading an interior life, the future will belong to Christianity.

M. D'HULST,<br>Rector of the Catholic Institute.

PARIS, *April 14th, 1882.*

# CONTENTS.

| CHAPTER | PAGE |
|---|---|
| I.—The Crib, | 1 |
| II.—The Angel and the Shepherds, | 4 |
| III.—Gloria In Excelsis Deo, | 7 |
| IV.—The Shepherds go to Bethlehem, | 10 |
| V.—The Adoration of the Shepherds, | 12 |
| VI.—The Star appears to the Magi, | 15 |
| VII.—The Kings prepare for their Journey, | 18 |
| VIII.—The Journey of the Kings, | 21 |
| IX.—The Kings at Jerusalem, | 24 |
| X.—The Child Jesus is adored by the Magi, | 27 |
| XI.—The Presentation in the Temple. Jesus is carried to Jerusalem, | 30 |
| XII.—The Presentation in the Temple, | 33 |
| XIII.—The Prophecy of Simeon, | 35 |
| XIV.—The Prophetess Anna blesses Jesus, | 38 |
| XV.—An Angel warns Joseph to fly into Egypt, | 40 |
| XVI.—The Flight into Egypt, | 43 |
| XVII.—The Flight into Egypt.—The Desert, | 46 |
| XVIII.—Arrival of the Holy Family in Egypt, | 49 |
| XIX.—The Holy Family seek a Shelter, | 52 |
| XX.—The Sojourn in Egypt, | 55 |
| XXI.—The Return to Galilee, | 57 |
| XXII.—The Arrival at Nazareth, | 60 |
| XXIII.—The Holy Family at Nazareth, | 62 |
| XXIV.—The Hidden Life at Nazareth, | 64 |
| XXV.—Jesus is taken to Jerusalem for the Pasch, | 66 |

| CHAPTER | PAGE |
|---|---|
| XXVI.—The Holy Family at Jerusalem, | 68 |
| XXVII.—Jesus is lost by His Parents, | 70 |
| XXVIII.—Mary and Joseph at Jerusalem, | 72 |
| XXIX.—The Finding of Jesus in the Temple, | 74 |
| XXX.—Jesus' Hidden Life at Nazareth, | 77 |
| XXXI.—Jesus works as a Carpenter, | 80 |
| XXXII.—Jesus leaves Nazareth, | 82 |
| XXXIII.—The Baptism of Jesus Christ, | 85 |
| XXXIV.—The Marriage Feast at Cana, | 88 |
| XXXV.—The Water changed to Wine, | 90 |
| XXXVI.—The Call of the Apostles, | 93 |
| XXXVII.—Jesus in the Bark of Simon, | 96 |
| XXXVIII.—Jesus casts the Sellers out of the Temple, | 99 |
| XXXIX.—The Zeal of Thy House hath eaten me up, | 102 |
| XL.—Nicodemus, | 104 |
| XLI.—Jacob's Well, | 106 |
| XLII.—The Samaritan Woman, | 108 |
| XLIII.—Jesus remains in Samaria, | 111 |
| XLIV.—The Ruler of Capharnaum seeks Jesus, | 113 |
| XLV.—The Ruler's Son is Cured, | 116 |
| XLVI.—Jesus cures St. Peter's Mother-in-law, | 118 |
| XLVII.—Jesus heals the Sick, | 121 |
| XLVIII.—Jesus Sleeps, | 124 |
| XLIX.—Jesus quells the Storm, | 126 |
| L.—The Cure of the Paralytic, | 128 |
| LI.—The Call of Saint Matthew, | 130 |
| LII.—The Hem of Jesus' Garment, | 133 |
| LIII.—The Raising of the Daughter of Jairus to Life, | 136 |
| LIV.—St. Mary Magdalen in Simon's House, | 139 |
| LV.—Jesus chooseth the Twelve Apostles, | 142 |
| LVI.—The Mission of the Apostles, | 145 |
| LVII.—The Centurion's Servant, | 148 |
| LVIII.—The Widow's Son, | 151 |

| CHAPTER | PAGE |
|---|---|
| LIX.—John's Two Disciples, | 154 |
| LX.—The Sower, | 157 |
| LXI.—The Rocky Soil, | 159 |
| LXII.—The Thorns and the good Ground, | 161 |
| LXIII.—Jesus and the Holy Women, | 163 |
| LXIV.—The Wheat and the Cockle, | 166 |
| LXV.—The Return of the Apostles, | 169 |
| LXVI.—The Crowd follow Jesus, | 171 |
| LXVII.—The Five Loaves, | 173 |
| LXVIII.—The Twelve Baskets, | 176 |
| LXIX.—Jesus Walking on the Water, | 178 |
| LXX.—Lord, save me! | 181 |
| LXXI.—To whom shall we go? | 184 |
| LXXII.—The Woman of Canaan, | 187 |
| LXXIII.—The Deaf and Dumb Man, | 190 |
| LXXIV.—The Blind Man of Bethsaida, | 193 |
| LXXV.—The Blind Man of Bethsaida.—*Continued*, | 195 |
| LXXVI.—Thou art the Christ, | 197 |
| LXXVII.—Blessed art thou, Simon Bar-Jona, | 199 |
| LXXVIII.—Jesus fortells His Sufferings, | 202 |
| LXXIX.—The Transfiguration, | 205 |
| LXXX.—The Three Tabernacles, | 208 |
| LXXXI.—Jesus descends from the Mountain, | 211 |
| LXXXII.—The Dumb Spirit, | 214 |
| LXXXIII.—Jesus casts out the Dumb Spirit, | 217 |
| LXXXIV.—Jesus payeth the Didrachma, | 220 |
| LXXXV.—Become as Little Children, | 223 |
| LXXXVI.—The Man born Blind, | 225 |
| LXXXVII.—The Faith of the Man born Blind, | 228 |
| LXXXVIII.—The Good Shepherd, | 231 |
| LXXXIX.—Mary and Martha, | 233 |
| XC.—The Rich Man, | 236 |
| XCI.—The Pharisees and Scribes murmur against Jesus, | 239 |

| CHAPTER | PAGE |
|---|---|
| XCII.—Lord, teach us to pray, | 242 |
| XCIII.—Zaccheus, | 245 |
| XCIV.—The Illness of Lazarus, | 248 |
| XCV.—The Illness of Lazarus.—Jesus' Return, | 251 |
| XCVI.—The Raising of Lazarus to Life, | 254 |
| XCVII.—The Disciples prepare the Pasch, | 257 |
| XCVIII.—Christ washeth His Disciples' Feet, | 260 |
| XCIX.—The Last Supper, | 263 |
| C.—Gethsemani, | 266 |
| CI.—The Traitor's Kiss, | 269 |
| CII.—The Blessed Virgin and St. John, | 272 |
| CIII.—Calvary, | 275 |
| CIV.—Jesus' Side is opened with a Spear, | 278 |
| CV.—The Return to Jerusalem, | 281 |
| CVI.—The Agonising Heart of Mary, | 284 |
| CVII.—The Resurrection, | 287 |

# FROM THE CRIB TO THE CROSS.

## CHAPTER I.

### THE CRIB.

And she brought forth her first born son, and wrapped him up in swaddling clothes, and laid him in a manger; because there was no room for them in the inn.—*St. Luke ii. 7.*

*Preparatory Prayer.* Help me, O my God, to keep my thoughts for a few moments from wandering, so that I may remain recollected in Thy presence and solely intent on Thee.

I. I am about to enter the cave at Bethlehem, which I desire to examine carefully and piously. It is midnight; the December night is cold, and dark, save for the light of the stars, which throw a few shadows round the Holy Spot. Within, a sweet celestial light plays around the Infant Jesus, and enables me to examine closely every detail of the cave, which is hewn out of the rock, and seems cold and damp.

II. Advancing a little farther, I place myself close to the Crib. Here what countless meditations, and lessons for us all! St. Ignatius, in his Spiritual Exercises, expresses the wish to stay there for ever, as the humblest servant of Jesus, Mary and Joseph. Why should not I also do the same? My God, I offer myself to Thee, as the lowliest of Thy servants.

III. The Infant Jesus is lying on the straw, while Mary bends lovingly over Him. Her face reveals her great joy, a joy which is nevertheless not unmingled with anxiety. This Blessed Babe, although her God, is yet her son. She loves and adores Him; but His intense poverty rends her maternal heart with grief. What should be my thoughts, when I behold my Saviour thus bereft of every thing, His only bed the cold and wretched straw? What grief should I not feel, were I to see the child of one dear to me, my baby brother for instance, having no other shelter than a cold damp cave, with only a poor manger for its cradle? Why do I not then feel the same pity for the Infant Jesus, my Divine Saviour?

When I think how great would be my mother's grief, were she to see one of her children in such a pitiful state, I can easily imagine the anguish which our Blessed Lady suffered at Bethlehem.

This consideration of the poverty of the Crib should remind me of the poverty of my heart, which, poor though it be, Jesus yet deigns to visit in Holy Communion. Is it not harder than the wood of the

# FROM THE CRIB TO THE CROSS.

## CHAPTER I.

### THE CRIB.

And she brought forth her first born son, and wrapped him up in swaddling clothes, and laid him in a manger; because there was no room for them in the inn.—*St. Luke ii. 7.*

*Preparatory Prayer.* Help me, O my God, to keep my thoughts for a few moments from wandering, so that I may remain recollected in Thy presence and solely intent on Thee.

I. I am about to enter the cave at Bethlehem, which I desire to examine carefully and piously. It is midnight; the December night is cold, and dark, save for the light of the stars, which throw a few shadows round the Holy Spot. Within, a sweet celestial light plays around the Infant Jesus, and enables me to examine closely every detail of the cave, which is hewn out of the rock, and seems cold and damp.

II. Advancing a little farther, I place myself close to the Crib. Here what countless meditations, and lessons for us all! St. Ignatius, in his Spiritual Exercises, expresses the wish to stay there for ever, as the humblest servant of Jesus, Mary and Joseph. Why should not I also do the same? My God, I offer myself to Thee, as the lowliest of Thy servants.

III. The Infant Jesus is lying on the straw, while Mary bends lovingly over Him. Her face reveals her great joy, a joy which is nevertheless not unmingled with anxiety. This Blessed Babe, although her God, is yet her son. She loves and adores Him; but His intense poverty rends her maternal heart with grief. What should be my thoughts, when I behold my Saviour thus bereft of every thing, His only bed the cold and wretched straw? What grief should I not feel, were I to see the child of one dear to me, my baby brother for instance, having no other shelter than a cold damp cave, with only a poor manger for its cradle? Why do I not then feel the same pity for the Infant Jesus, my Divine Saviour?

When I think how great would be my mother's grief, were she to see one of her children in such a pitiful state, I can easily imagine the anguish which our Blessed Lady suffered at Bethlehem.

This consideration of the poverty of the Crib should remind me of the poverty of my heart, which, poor though it be, Jesus yet deigns to visit in Holy Communion. Is it not harder than the wood of the manger, colder than the rocks, where I behold Thee, my God, stretched on the comfortless straw?

IV. Turning now towards St. Joseph, I notice that, after adoring the Infant Jesus, his next care is to make his God's first shelter on earth less cold and uncomfortable. An ox and an ass are the sole other occupants of this wretched stable; these he brings nearer to the Divine Child, that they may warm Him by their breath. He then makes some sort of a door to keep out the cold night wind.

I too, like St. Joseph, will try to render my heart less cold, less devoid of good dispositions, and better prepared to receive Jesus. Not only then at the moment of Holy Communion will I endeavour to be devout; but since even small sacrifices are pleasing to our Lord, I will resolve, before taking leave of the Crib, so poor and comfortless, to offer Him all the little vexations I have to bear, as well as the efforts necessary to overcome myself on such occasions.

*Resolution.* I will offer to Jesus every morning, at my prayers, all my actions of the day, and ask Him to give me the strength I need; and then, should any small trouble arise, I will remember that a little sacrifice on my part will console Jesus, Mary and Joseph, for what they endured at Bethlehem, and I will most gladly accept it for their sakes.

*Prayer.* O Mary, receive my resolutions, offer them to Jesus, ask Him to bless them, and to make me persevere.

## CHAPTER II.

### THE ANGEL AND THE SHEPHERDS.

And there were in the same country shepherds watching, and keeping the night-watches over their flock.

And behold, an Angel of the Lord stood by them, and the brightness of God shone round about them, and they feared with a great fear.

And the Angel said to them: Fear not; for behold I bring you good tidings of great joy, that shall be to all the people.

For this day is born to you a Saviour, who is Christ the Lord, in the city of David.

And this shall be a sign unto you: You shall find the infant wrapped in swaddling clothes, and laid in a manger. —*St. Luke ii. 8 to 12.*

*Preparatory Prayer.* Help me, my God, to make a good meditation, and to consecrate to Thee all my thoughts and resolutions.

I. I will picture to myself the plains of Judea, the calm starlight night, the shepherds watching their flocks. I can easily understand the alarm of these poor simple peasants, when they suddenly perceive a brilliant light, and an Angel appears in the sky. What is he about to announce? Does he bring tidings of life or of death? These poor people tremble and are about to beg for mercy. Oh! be comforted! You do not as yet understand the gentleness of Jesus, but soon you will learn to know Him, in listening to the first words of peace and hope, which His Advent brings to men. "Fear not," said the Angel. O my dear Saviour, to me also dost Thou address these words by the mouth of Thy heavenly messenger.

Fear not. Courage, my child, God is a kind, a tender Father; He should be served with the loving obedience of a child to its mother. Courage.

I should then never be discouraged, no matter what difficulty I may have in correcting my faults. God will always be with me, my efforts will be counted. Courage.

II. I will continue to listen to the words of the Angel: "For this day is born to you a Saviour, Who is Christ the Lord, in the city of David. And this shall be a sign unto you: you shall find the infant wrapped in swaddling clothes and laid in a manger." The very helplessness of Jesus is then the foundation of my confidence. He wished to be my Saviour, and to redeem me He took upon Himself my poor weak nature. He knows how, in spite of all my good resolutions, my weakness yields to the first little difficulty. He knows well my misery and has compassion on my frailty. He suffered in order to help me to suffer, to work, to struggle against my faults.

Courage then, I will press onward, leaning for support on Jesus Himself.

*Resolution.* I know that after many efforts, many good resolutions, a mere trifle will often suffice to distract me and make me relapse into my ordinary faults; but with God's help I will never be discouraged. When I feel inclined to yield to temptation, I will consider how the sweet Child Jesus chose to be helpless and weak, incapable of the slightest movement without the assistance of His mother, who carried Him in her arms. I will place all my confidence in the Divine Child, begging of Mary, His Mother and mine, to take me also in her loving arms.

*Prayer.* From this moment forward, O most tender Mother, I place myself under thy protection, and I beseech thee from my heart to watch over me unceasingly. O Mary, show thyself my Mother.

## CHAPTER III.

### GLORIA IN EXCELSIS DEO.

And suddenly, there was with the Angel a multitude of the heavenly army, praising God, and saying:
Glory to God in the highest, and on earth peace to men of goodwill.—*St. Luke ii. 13 and 14.*

*Preparatory Prayer.* Grant me, my God, the grace of holy recollection, during this short meditation, that I may forget all else but Thee alone.

I. I will remain in spirit with the shepherds, who have been awakened from slumber by the joyful news of our Saviour's birth, announced by the Angel.

The celestial light surrounding this beautiful vision enables them to perceive in the starlit sky a brilliant host of heavenly spirits hovering above them: I can picture them to myself gazing enraptured on this company of bright spirits in the azure vault. The hearts of these poor men are filled with joy; they are deeply moved by the heavenly vision, and by the sweet melody that is borne in upon their ears.

"Glory be to God on high, and on earth peace to men of goodwill," sing the angels joyfully.

It is the song of triumph with which God Himself has inspired His messengers, in order to make known the birth of His Son.

II. Here let me pause for a while and consider these blessed words: "Glory be to God." To glorify God is the sole occupation of the angels in Heaven. They teach us that we who are on earth should unite with them in giving glory to the Divine Omnipotence.

But how can creatures so small, so humble as we, give glory to the great God? The life and teachings of our dear Saviour show us how; there is no creature, no matter how frail, that has not its share of glory to render to God. Dear Lord, I who am so weak, so powerless, so young, what can I do to glorify Thee?

I seem to hear our Lord reply: "Be faithful to thy duties, obey thy parents and those who hold their place, have great confidence in thy mother, be straightforward in all thy ways, bear patiently to be forgotten and paid no attention to: these are the means in thy power to glorify God." But how can I hope to acquire these virtues, knowing myself to be so weak? The continuation of the angels' song instructs and consoles me. "Peace on earth to men of goodwill." It is therefore goodwill alone that can give us peace, and God must value it highly, since He proclaims its efficacy by the mouth of His Angel at the very moment of our Saviour's birth.

*Resolution.* From henceforth I will endeavour to cultivate a firm goodwill, that it may increase daily in my heart, according as years alter the nature of my duties, and multiply my opportunities of giving glory to God. And as, in order to have goodwill, I must above all pray for it, I resolve to-day, O my dear Saviour, to say often: "Lord, give me a sincere goodwill."

*Prayer.* Grant me, O my God, grace to acquire the habit of frequently addressing to Thee this prayer; and do ye, O holy angels, who sang the heavenly hymn that announced the birth of Jesus, obtain for me, I beseech you, the precious gift of goodwill.

## CHAPTER IV.

### THE SHEPHERDS GO TO BETHLEHEM.

And it came to pass, after the angels departed from them into heaven, the shepherds said one to another : Let us go over to Bethlehem, and let us see this word that is come to pass, which the Lord hath showed to us.—*St. Luke ii. 15.*

*Preparatory Prayer.* Behold me, my God, most earnestly desirous of recollecting myself in Thy presence; grant me the grace to understand the lessons Thou teachest, and to put them in practice.

I. The angels' song has ceased, and all is silent once more in Bethlehem and the surrounding country. I picture to myself the shepherds, amazed at the tidings announced by the heavenly messenger, asking each other with astonishment, if all had been witnesses of the marvel.

Will they be content to remain lost in wonder? Will they await the dawn of day to endeavour to know something more of the birth of Christ? Before seeking Him, will they not try to find out if anyone has yet beheld Him? No; these simple peasants are docile to the words of the Angel. "Let us go over to Bethlehem," said they, "and they came with haste," adds the Holy Gospel.

II. In their readiness, I should find a practical

lesson for myself. Have I not also an angel who whispers to me warnings sent by God? Has he not spoken to me many times by the voice of my conscience, and have I always listened with docility to his admonitions? Young as I am, and preserved by my age and the tender watchfulness of my parents, from the great difficulties of life, there is yet often within me a struggle between good and evil. Each act of submission nearly always costs me a great effort, which is due to the strife going on, and the danger I am in of basely yielding.

*Resolution.* As a fruit of these reflections I resolve to follow unhesitatingly the promptings of grace, without giving time for other impressions to weaken my resolution and tempt me to draw back.

*Prayer.* Dear angel, my faithful companion, thou who watchest over me so well, obtain for me, I entreat, the habit of obeying promptly, without hesitation, the good inspirations dictated by thee.

## CHAPTER V.

### THE ADORATION OF THE SHEPHERDS.

And they came with haste: and they found Mary and Joseph, and the infant lying in a manger.

And seeing, they understood of the word that had been spoken to them concerning this child.—*St. Luke ii. 16 and 17.*

*Preparatory Prayer.* My God, I offer Thee my mind and my heart.

I. I return in spirit to the cave of Bethlehem. There I behold the Divine Child Jesus with Mary and Joseph. Before them kneel the shepherds humbly. Mary, in her goodness, wishes to make them adore her dear Son Jesus, Whom she has taken on her knees, as she invites them to approach. Her sweet and beautiful countenance beams with joy and gratitude. She looks alternately from her precious treasure to the humble shepherds kneeling at His Feet. Saint Joseph, too, is there, and is no doubt full of kindness towards the poor men, whom he willingly allows to enter the cave, and approach the Holy Child and His Mother.

II. Is not this, O my God, a type of what awaits me each time that I seek Thee by prayer, or kneel before Thy tabernacle? Is not Mary there also to present me to Jesus? Will Joseph listen less readily to my petition than to that of the shepherds at the

Crib? O Mary, O Joseph, I beg of you this day to present me to Jesus; teach me to offer Him, with perfect simplicity, my heart and my good intentions.

III. If I were but fully convinced of this truth, that Jesus is as really present in the tabernacle as in the Crib, how much more fervent would I be, and with what devotion would I tell Him of my love!

I will endeavour to understand the feelings of the shepherds, so that I may imitate them. Their looks betray what is passing in their hearts. They are awed and recollected in the presence of their Saviour; their docility in obeying the Angel has merited for them the grace of a lively faith. But this is not all. Make me understand, O my God, the grandeur of the scene that is taking place in this poor stable; heaven itself descends into this humble abode; millions of bright angels surround the Crib, and without ever leaving the throne of the Most High, annihilate themselves before the Child God. What reflections should not this beautiful thought inspire in me, did I but know how to meditate better! How much greater would be my respect after Holy Communion, did I but understand the profound adoration of the angels! For is it not the same Redeemer and God Who comes to dwell within me? When He deigns to enter my heart, numberless angels surround me to adore Him. And I, where are my thoughts, where my faith, where my acts of praise? Oh! how this thought confounds and humbles me!

*Resolution.* I will imitate the faith of the shepherds, the devotion of the angels at Bethlehem, and will henceforth redouble my respect and love after Holy Communion; I will converse as long as possible with Jesus, Mary and Joseph, and I will repeat the acts after Holy Communion slowly, and paying due attention to each word.

*Prayer.* O my God, grant me the grace never to forget this resolution; Mary, my dear Mother, teach me how to receive and adore Jesus in my heart.

## CHAPTER VI.

### THE STAR APPEARS TO THE MAGI.

For we have seen his star in the East, and are come to adore him.—*St. Matt. ii. 2.*

*Preparatory Prayer.* O my God, watch, I beseech Thee, over my senses, so prone to distractions, and grant that my thoughts may be of Thee alone.

I. Our Lord had been adored by poor shepherds; He now calls to His cradle powerful kings. He blesses all stations in life, and loves all submissive hearts. I will consider the three Magi surrounded by a numerous court. The ties of relationship, worldly goods, the authority they possess, all is calculated to keep them in their own country. Nevertheless, a marvellous event calls them from afar; the birth of Jesus is revealed to them by the foretold apparition of a star, which was to guide them on their journey. How great must have been their fidelity to grace, thus to quit all and follow the star. What opposition must they not have encountered. Their undertaking was probably blamed, called rash and foolish. Most likely their relations made use of every means in their power to hinder their departure. In those days journeys were not so easy as they now are. Great preparations were necessary, a numerous retinue, camels, tents, troops of sheep and oxen to feed the travellers. And, once started on the journey, no means of communication with those they had left behind. No matter, their faith is lively, they are resolved to set out. Perhaps other princes, weaker and more cowardly than they, conceived the same project, but had not the courage to carry it into execution.

II. Should I not here examine myself? Have I not often abandoned the good resolutions which I had formed? Has not a slight objection or a remark, made in my presence, been sufficient sometimes to prevent my carrying out my good intention? How shameful to think that I have allowed myself to be influenced by human respect, and oh, what danger for the future! I am now sheltered from real difficulties, by reason of my age and the tender care which watches over me. If already a simple criticism is sufficient to shake my resolution, how shall I, later in life, resist the temptation of bad example?

*Resolution.* When I am criticised for some pious practice, or blamed for some little act of charity or some good action of which my superiors approve, I will persevere courageously. When I am offered a drive, a party of pleasure, or some other gratification which would interfere with a pious plan already formed, I will let my superiors decide for me, without manifesting too great eagerness for the proposed pleasure. By these little victories over myself, I will endeavour to become more pleasing to God, and make His Will my first object.

*Prayer.* O sweet Infant Jesus, help my weakness, bless Thy child who offers Thee these resolutions at the foot of Thy Crib.

# CHAPTER VII.

## THE KINGS PREPARE FOR THEIR JOURNEY.

When Jesus, therefore, was born in Bethlehem of Juda, in the days of King Herod, behold, there came wise men from the East to Jerusalem.—*St. Matthew ii. 1.*

*Preparatory Prayer.* Dear Saviour, behold me at Thy Feet, bless me, receive my good intentions, take possession of my thoughts and of my imagination, so easily led astray.

I. I have seen how faithful were the Kings in answering God's call, and how they at once decided to set out. There were, however, many things to be done before they could put their resolution into effect. I will consider, in the first place, the joy of these good Magi, who are filled with rapture at the thought of going to seek their Saviour; they plan together what offerings they will bring Him; they converse with joy about the object of their journey. Around them all is in motion; their servants and retinue are making ready; a large purchase of tents and provisions is being made; all are occupied going to and fro on various errands.

How many in all this crowd understand the blessing announced by the star? These men are obedient to their masters, but what is passing in the depths of their hearts? Some mechanically fulfil the duties of their different offices; others derive great amusement from the preparations for a journey which excites their curiosity, but by far the greater number are opposed to the idea. Many openly murmur at the distance they have to go; others are discontented without daring to manifest their annoyance. What an amount of criticisms must not this out-of-the-way expedition have evoked!

II. This is what still occurs in our own days. The time, the country, the events are no longer the same, but it is always the same picture of human weakness, and in this picture I behold my own faults. How often I allow myself to criticise the actions of those whom I ought to respect! I will at once examine myself seriously on this point, and will endeavour to amend.

*Resolution.* When such a one, perhaps my brother or sister, expresses thoughts and feelings different to my own; when I see in some other family, ways unlike those I am accustomed to, I will be careful not to criticise. I will remember that I have too often found fault with persons far better than myself, perhaps because I did not feel disposed to imitate their virtues. I will carefully avoid this base and cowardly feeling. When I see what is really worthy of blame, I will be silent, remembering that, at my age, I am incapable of forming a just opinion, and that, at all ages, we are forbidden to judge others.

*Prayer.* O my God, grant me the grace never to abandon the pious practices of my childhood; teach me also to admire and imitate those who are better than myself, whilst I pity and pray for those who have not received so many graces.

## CHAPTER VIII.

### THE JOURNEY OF THE KINGS.

. . . Behold, there came wise men from the East to Jerusalem.—*St. Matthew ii. 1.*

*Preparatory Prayer.* Make me, my God, attentive and recollected; I place myself most specially under Thy protection, and I consecrate to Thee all my thoughts.

I. The Kings have now started on their journey, guided by the miraculous star. They are only three in number, but their retinue forms an immense caravan, stretching far away out of sight along the winding road. The path is not so easy as those I have been accustomed to. I can therefore readily imagine that the journey must sometimes be very fatiguing; the heavily laden camels, the men on horseback, and the numerous animals, taken as provisions for the travellers, are often obliged to proceed one by one, so narrow is the way.

Sometimes, too, they suffer from thirst, that most cruel of all torments, which travellers in those far-off countries have to endure. As there are certainly, amongst the followers of the Magi, many who hold different opinions as to the advisability of the journey, those who are against it must be very angry and discontented, when the fatigue becomes excessive. How heavy a burden must they then be to their companions!

II. Do not these discontented followers of the Kings suggest to me this practical reflection. How often have I acted in the same manner, showing my discontent, and not even endeavouring to hide my vexation, when things did not go exactly as I wished, and that, not only, when I was forced to obey in matters that cost me an effort, but often, even when my wishes were granted, or because every thing was not just as I would like? For instance, should the enjoyment of a party of pleasure, a game, or a holiday, be marred by some slight *contretemps*, it would seem as though I had a right to find fault with everybody, and to be in a bad temper with all around me.

*Resolution.* I will henceforth endeavour to become gentle and even-tempered, always looking upon the bright side of things, in spite of contradictions and annoyances. Let me reflect too, whither all these malcontents are journeying. They little know the grace that awaits them at their destination. To see the Child Jesus, to know Him, to adore Him, to be loved by Him! And I also, each time that I conquer my bad temper, that I remain unruffled in spite of vexations, contradictions, or disappointments, I too, shall find Jesus! He will whisper in the depths of my heart a word of sweetest consolation; my conscience will tell me that Jesus is pleased with me. What joy! What peace!

*Prayer.* O my dear Saviour, penetrate me with this thought, so that when occasion shall arise, I may be faithful to my resolution.

## CHAPTER IX.

### THE KINGS AT JERUSALEM.

. . . Behold, there came wise men from the East to Jerusalem,

Saying, Where is he that is born King of the Jews? For we have seen his star in the East, and are come to adore him.

And King Herod, hearing this, was troubled, and all Jerusalem with him.

And assembling together all the chief priests and the Scribes of the people, he inquired of them where Christ should be born.

But they said to him: In Bethlehem of Juda. For so it is written by the prophet.

And thou Bethlehem the land of Juda art not the least among the princes of Juda: for out of thee shall come forth the captain that shall rule my people Israel.

Then Herod privately calling the wise men learned diligently of them the time of the star which appeared to them;

And sending them into Bethlehem, said: Go and diligently inquire after the child, and when you have found him, bring me word again, that I also may come and adore him.

Who having heard the king, went their way; and behold the star which they had seen in the East, went before them, until it came and stood over where the child was.

And seeing the star they rejoiced with exceeding great joy.
—*St. Matthew ii. 1-10.*

*Preparatory Prayer.* I wish, O my Jesus, to consecrate to Thee all my thoughts. Help me, I beseech

Thee, for Thou knowest with what difficulty I remain recollected, even at Thy Sacred Feet.

I. I have witnessed in spirit the departure of the Magi, and followed them on their journey. At last their caravan reaches Jerusalem. The astonished inhabitants behold with wonder this splendid cortege as it enters the town; the long array of camels, the numerous retinue, the three Kings together, surrounded by a large court; never before have they witnessed such a sight. The streets are crowded with men and women; children flock from all parts, and are enchanted with the brilliant spectacle: they gaze open-mouthed on the camels laden with presents, and caparisoned in the most elegant and costly manner, and on the richly coloured stuffs of their trappings.

II. Herod on his part is troubled, for he is informed of the arrival of the strangers; he wishes to find out the meaning of the splendid cortege, and therefore offers hospitality in his own name to the new comers.

As to the Magi, they have not hitherto felt the slightest uneasiness, for they have unhesitatingly followed the star. Now an unexpected trial awaits them; the star disappears. Do these pious Kings become faint-hearted? Do they yield to feelings of discouragement? No, no, their faith is not shaken; they seek counsel from the doctors of the law; and when they are told that the prophets have designated Bethlehem as the birthplace of the Messiah, they eagerly hasten thither, without doubt, hesitation, or argument; they obey without delay. A joyful surprise awaits them; scarcely have they quitted Jerusalem, when the star again appears. Oh, what rapture must they not have felt, to see it once more, shining as brightly as at the commencement of their journey! I can fancy them going one to the other, asking if all had seen the welcome sight, and thanking God for thus rewarding their docility.

*Resolution.* I will consider how happy I am in knowing so well what I ought to do, since, at my age, I have only to obey without hesitation. I will learn to love obedience, even when it costs me most.

*Prayer.* What a good and generous Master art Thou, O my God! Thou never failest to reward the docile heart. Penetrate me deeply with this truth, Lord Jesus, and make me always Thy obedient child.

---

## CHAPTER X.

### THE CHILD JESUS IS ADORED BY THE MAGI.

And entering into the house, they found the Child with Mary his mother, and falling down they adored him, and opening their treasures, they offered him gifts ; gold, frankincense, and myrrh.—*St. Matthew ii. 11.*

*Preparatory Prayer.* Bless, O Lord, my thoughts and resolutions, and grant me the grace to consecrate them all to Thee.

I. I am again in spirit at the Crib, and joyfully approach my infant Saviour. Mary is still occupied with the sweet care of her Divine Son.

Several days have elapsed since His birth, and the cave of Bethlehem, in spite of St. Joseph's efforts to render it more habitable, is still very poor and miserable. The shepherds and neighbouring villagers have nevertheless brought some branches of trees, some moss and straw ; and the presence of Jesus and Mary renders this poor stable the richest of earthly habitations. The heart of the Blessed Virgin is filled with joy and faith, as she contemplates her Divine Child slumbering peacefully in her arms. Of a sudden an unwonted sound is heard in the distance, at first confused, but gradually becoming more and more distinct.

Exclamations of joy, mingled with the sound of footsteps and the trampling of horses, are borne in on Mary's ear. She knows that fresh homage is about to be offered to the Child Jesus, and, as she listens, the strangers enter the cave. Oh, what emotion must not these pious Kings have felt, when they found themselves in presence of this Babe, Who was also their God! Mary having graciously permitted them to approach, they gaze with rapture on the sweet Child Jesus, smiling in His sleep, and seeming to invite their adoration.

II. But the Magi are not satisfied with simply adoring the Infant Jesus, they have brought rich treasures from afar, which they joyfully lay at His Feet. The Gospel tells us that opening their treasures, they offered Him gold, frankincense, and myrrh. They offered Him gold, emblem of riches, because He was their King, the King of heaven and earth; incense in virtue of His Godhead, for incense was always burned at sacrifices; and myrrh, symbol of humanity, the perfume used to embalm the dead, because of the human nature which He had vouchsafed to take upon Himself.

*Resolution.* When I behold the Magi thus offering their gifts, I will reflect upon a salutary thought suggested by a pious author (Père Nouët). We have followed the Magi in spirit to the Feet of Jesus, shall we remain there empty-handed? Oh, no! dear Lord, I too wish to offer Thee something, and yet what can I give, where can I find a treasure to present to Thee!

I have nothing to give but my heart, and this I now gladly lay before Thee, and offer to Thee entirely with all its affections. Deign to receive it, Lord Jesus, bless it and take it into Thy safe keeping. May it be always Thine alone.

*Prayer.* O Holy Child Jesus, I give Thee my heart by the hands of Mary, Thy Mother and mine.

## CHAPTER XI.

### THE PRESENTATION IN THE TEMPLE. JESUS IS CARRIED TO JERUSALEM.

And after the days of her purification according to the law of Moses were accomplished, they carried him to Jerusalem, to present him to the Lord.—*St. Luke ii. 22.*

*Preparatory Prayer.* My God, grant me the grace to profit by this meditation, and to understand Thy Divine teaching.

I. For the first time, our Blessed Lady leaves the Crib. That poor but peaceful and hallowed spot is no doubt very dear to her, and I can easily imagine that she quits it with regret; Mary has however already commenced the life of constant sacrifice, which is to be her portion on earth.

But in leaving Bethlehem, the Blessed Virgin does not quit her beloved Babe; she carries Him in her arms with profound reverence. How fondly she presses Him to her bosom! Jesus is silent, but oh, what secrets does he not whisper to Mary's heart!

When I received Him for the first time in Holy Communion, what silence reigned within me, and yet what sweet converse my soul held with God! Mary wears a long flowing veil, in the folds of which she wraps the Child Jesus, the most beautiful among the sons of men according to the language of Holy Scripture. St. Joseph carries the two doves, which poor people were obliged, according to the law, to offer as the ransom of their new-born child. His noble countenance contrasts strangely with the poverty of his garments, and the roughness of his hands accustomed to toil.

II. Perhaps as the Holy Family ascend the steps leading to the Temple, they meet persons of high rank, coming down. Who could have told that these poor people stepping humbly aside to let their richer brethren pass by, had with them the God of heaven and earth? Mary and Joseph know it well, but they pass unnoticed, happy in the treasure they possess, though in no wise seeking their own glorification.

What a subject for reflection is here. If the position of my parents is superior to that of others, I will try to remain simple, knowing that this is not a subject of merit, as far as I am concerned. What right indeed have I to be proud of that which is God's free gift? At my age one is apt to think a great deal of one's own importance, and nothing is more displeasing to God than that stupid pride which makes a merit of gifts, so entirely gratuitous. If, on the contrary, my position is humble, I will drive far from me all feelings of envy: I will think of the Holy Family, and remember with gratitude that our Lord chose to be born poor, in order to help me to bear my poverty.

*Resolution.* I will be careful how I act towards my neighbours. I will try and treat everyone as the Blessed Virgin would have done, to be respectful to my superiors, affable to my equals, and kind to my inferiors.

*Prayer.* O my God, I thank Thee for the position in life which Thou hast prepared for me from all eternity: may my gratitude for this favour help me to love Thee with all my heart.

## CHAPTER XII.

### THE PRESENTATION IN THE TEMPLE.

. . . They carried him to Jerusalem, to present him to the Lord,

. . . . . . . . . .

And to offer a sacrifice according as it is written in the law of the Lord, a pair of turtle doves, or two young pigeons.—*St. Luke ii. 22 and 24.*

*Preparatory Prayer.* Fill my soul, O God, with Thy Holy Grace, so that I may understand the gift of Himself which Jesus makes Thee, and endeavour to imitate it.

I. I behold the Infant Jesus offered by His parents to Almighty God, that He may be consecrated to Him. God loves first fruits, and according to the Jewish law all first-born children were to be given to Him. These children were ransomed, for the rich, by two lambs, for the poor, by two doves. Mary is poor, she therefore offers doves. How happy is the fate of these little birds about to be sacrificed to God. I will contemplate Mary, as she raises her eyes to the Holy of Holies, and offers to God from the depths of her heart her Divine Child. I will consider Jesus sweetly slumbering in the Blessed Virgin's arms. He offers Himself out of love for me, to obtain my salvation, in doing the Will of His Heavenly Father. I, too, have been consecrated to God in holy baptism, but do I really belong to Him? He loves first fruits. Have I been careful to dedicate to His glory these first years of my life?

When He asks of me some little sacrifice, do I make it generously?

II. At this supreme moment, not a word is spoken, but the hearts of those present are full to overflowing. Saint Joseph contemplates the joyful scene: Mary unites herself to the Child Jesus, Whose very presence in the Temple, proclaims loudly: "I am come, O Lord, to do Thy Will." It is not by words that we should glorify God, it is by actions. In thus obeying the precept of the law, Jesus, Mary and Joseph, are all most perfectly fulfilling the Will of God.

*Resolution.* I will endeavour to-day to unite all my actions with those of the Child Jesus, so that I may be able to say with Him: "I am come, O my God, to do Thy Will."

*Prayer.* O Jesus, I offer Thee the first fruits of my life; bless them, and grant me the grace to always do God's holy Will.

## CHAPTER XIII.

### THE PROPHECY OF SIMEON.

And behold there was a man in Jerusalem named Simeon, and this man was just and devout, waiting for the consolation of Israel, and the Holy Ghost was in him.

And he had received an answer from the Holy Ghost, that he should not see death before he had seen the Christ of the Lord.

And he came by the Spirit into the temple. And when his parents brought in the child Jesus, to do for him according to the custom of the law:

He also took him into his arms, and blessed God, and said:

Now thou dost dismiss thy servant, O Lord, according to thy word in peace:

Because my eyes have seen thy salvation,

Which thou hast prepared before the face of all peoples.

A light to the revelation of the gentiles, and the glory of thy people Israel.

And his father and mother were wondering at those things which were spoken concerning him.

And Simeon blessed them, and said to Mary his mother: Behold this child is set for the fall, and for the resurrection of many in Israel, and for a sign which shall be contradicted:

And thy own soul a sword shall pierce, that out of many hearts thoughts may be revealed.—*St. Luke ii. 25-35.*

*Preparatory Prayer.* Behold me, Lord, at Thy Feet. Deign to speak to my heart, and make me attentive to the slightest actions of Jesus, Mary and Joseph.

I. I will again consider the Holy Family, as they enter the Temple, that beautiful and magnificent building, whose splendours surpass the power of my imagination.

To have even the slightest idea of its grandeur, I must think of all the most magnificent things I have ever beheld; profusions of rare marbles, splendid gilding, and brightly coloured mosaics abound. Moreover, a most delicious subtle perfume seems to float upon the air.

Mary and the humble Joseph advance with the most profound reverence, for is not Jesus with them? I will consider attentively the scene which I am about to witness, and will endeavour to draw profit from it. Scarcely has the Divine Child crossed the threshold of the Temple, when Simeon, in a transport of joy, takes Him from His Mother's arms and sings his "Nunc Dimittis."

This joyful canticle, which breaks from Simeon's lips, expresses the gratitude with which his heart is filled to overflowing.

What an imposing sight is that on which I gaze! The holy old man, whose venerable countenance and long white beard contrast with the tender Babe clasped in his arms; Jesus, Who looks lovingly upon him; Mary, who, though never weary of contemplating her beloved Son, has nevertheless allowed Simeon to take Him from her, for she is always ready to share with others the sweet joy of Jesus' presence.

She listens to the old man's words fortelling the sword of sorrow which is to pierce her heart, and humbly accepts the sad prospect. This very canticle of Simeon's is sung every Sunday at Compline: for 1800 years these words have been repeated from mouth to mouth, and from generation to generation.

II. Why have I hitherto never reflected upon the grandeur of our holy religion? With what dispositions have I generally assisted at Vespers and Compline? Do I not yield to constant voluntary distractions? The Divine Office wearies me, and I do not even try to be recollected. And yet, if I but considered how grand are the prayer-like psalms of David, inspired by Almighty God, and sung by countless generations, the *Magnificat*, pronounced by Mary herself, and the *Nunc Dimittis*, which greeted my Saviour on His entry into the Temple, how ashamed should I be of my carelessness!

*Resolution.* I will resolve to learn the meaning of the Prayers used by the Church.

*Prayer.* O my God, forgive my heedlessness; teach me Thyself, I beg of Thee, to understand the sublimity of the Church's prayers, and make me assist with great recollectedness at the beautiful ceremonies of our holy religion.

## CHAPTER XIV.

### THE PROPHETESS ANNA BLESSES JESUS.

And there was one Anna a prophetess, the daughter of Phanuel, of the tribe of Aser: she was far advanced in years, and had lived with her husband seven years from her virginity.

And she was a widow until four-score and four years: who departed not from the temple, by fastings and prayers serving night and day.

Now she at the same hour coming in, confessed to the Lord: and spoke of him to all that looked for the redemption of Israel.—*St. Luke ii. 36 to 38.*

*Preparatory Prayer.* Make me truly recollected, O my God, so that I may learn to know Thee better and love Thee more.

I. Whilst Simeon foretells the sufferings that are one day to pierce Mary's heart, a woman of advanced years enters the Temple to praise the Lord. She also is to be a witness that the Messiah has come. God has spoken to her heart, and she knows that this little helpless Child is the Saviour of mankind. But who is this privileged woman? She is eighty-four years of age, and has led a life of singular holiness, having long served God in prayer, fasting and works of charity. Her cheeks are furrowed with privations and long vigils. And yet the Prophetess Anna, for it she, is happy. Despite her age, her crippled state, and her infirmities which are sufficiently great to allow her to relax her austerities, she is happy. For this life, which has perhaps been blamed and sometimes laughed at, called foolish and exaggerated,—so easily is that which is holy, judged by those who are not holy,—this very life gains for her the privilege of understanding the sublime scene at which she is present. How sweetly Mary welcomes her! When Simeon restores the Divine Infant to His Holy Mother, I almost think I see her hastening to place Him in Anna's arms.

II. This touching scene should teach me a practical lesson. I know many pious people, who spend long hours in church, who live retired from the world, and frequently approach the Sacraments. Have I not often felt inclined to look upon such persons as exaggerated and tiresome, without even exactly knowing why? It is an instinct, a sort of natural inclination: one does not like what is better than oneself. And yet such a person leading this kind of life, is probably a very privileged soul, and very dear to Mary.

*Resolution.* I will conquer this unworthy feeling, whenever I discover it in myself, by reflecting that the Child Jesus loves souls that seek Him with so much perseverance: and I will try, from to-day, to seek God, first of all in my prayers, and then in the work which is the duty of my state of life.

*Prayer.* Make me, O my God, faithful in seeking Thee, like Anna, with zeal and perseverance.

## CHAPTER XV.

### AN ANGEL WARNS JOSEPH TO FLY INTO EGYPT.

*And after they were departed, behold an Angel of the Lord appeared in sleep to Joseph, saying: Arise, and take the child and his mother, and fly into Egypt, and be there until I shall tell thee. For it will come to pass that Herod will seek the child to destroy him.—St. Matt. ii. 13.*

*Preparatory Prayer.* Lord, speak to my heart, that it may listen to and love Thee.

I. The Gospel tells me that an angel appeared to Joseph during the night. His slumber no doubt was heavy, for he had worked all day to provide the Holy Family with the necessaries of life. I behold him, therefore, sleeping the sound sleep of a poor tired labourer. But before taking his repose, he has not failed to address a fervent prayer to God, and has made sure that all around him is at rest, and that no danger threatens the humble dwelling of the King of heaven and earth. O Joseph, thou hast prayed, God therefore watches doubly over His Son and over thee! Nevertheless, danger is close at hand. For the first time the Infant Jesus is in peril: but an angel keeps watch over Him, and says to Joseph: "Arise, and take the Child and His Mother, and fly into Egypt."

II. Joseph hears the voice from heaven, and, rising

in haste, at once obeys the messenger of God. And yet how painful must it not have been to cause Mary such grief, by telling her that the persecution has already commenced, and that Jesus' life is threatened? Still he obeys. O Mary, and you too, O Joseph, make me understand how sad was that night of sudden awakening and hasty departure!

I will consider the obedience of the Blessed Virgin, making all possible haste, without losing her sweet peaceful serenity. Her first impulse was, no doubt, to clasp in her arms her persecuted Jesus, to press Him to her heart, so as to prove her love and, at the same time, shelter Him from danger. But this movement of our Blessed Lady was also inspired by another feeling, which should serve me for a lesson and example. To clasp Jesus, and press Him to one's heart in the hour of danger, is to have recourse to Him, and therein lies the true secret of Christian fortitude. With Jesus, all things are easy. Oh! how deeply convinced of this truth ought we not to be, in order to fight bravely against dangers and sorrows! And it is not only in great difficulties that we should call Jesus to our aid, draw close to Him, and address to Him our loving prayers. I am too young to have great trials, my sorrows are proportioned to my strength; but I will remember that to great courage are sent great trials, to little courage, little trials.

*Resolution.* In my small troubles, when, for instance, my studies tire me, when obedience becomes distasteful and I am a prey to *ennui*, when temptations to idleness and insubordination come upon me, I will clasp Jesus, that is to say, I will draw near in spirit to Mary, and ask her to give me Jesus, to let me press Him to my heart, that He may be my strength, my courage, and my consolation.

*Prayer.* O Jesus, strength of Mary and Joseph, strengthen me and help me in all my difficulties.

## CHAPTER XVI.

### THE FLIGHT INTO EGYPT.

Who arose, and took the child and his mother by night, and retired into Egypt.—*St. Matthew* ii. 14.

*Preparatory Prayer.* O Child Jesus, I ardently desire to know and love Thee with all my heart: bless, I pray Thee, my good intention, and make me very attentive to what I am about to read.

I. Joseph has obeyed, and the Holy Family have set out. But whither are they journeying? Has Joseph any friends or relations in the distant country to which he is going, or will he find there the means of earning a livelihood? Where will he find a shelter for Jesus and Mary? He knows not. Oh! what painful reflections must have presented themselves to the mind of Joseph, but each new thought only makes him renew his acts of faith and confidence! His eyes rest lovingly upon Jesus, the sight of Whom sustains his courage, and enables him to continue fearlessly on his way. The fatigue of the journey, was probably all the greater because, owing to the necessity for concealment, the more frequented roads had to be avoided, and in those days the mountain paths of Judea were rough and stony. I can fancy the narrow passes, the dangerous footpaths, in a word, all the fatigue and weariness of the holy travellers.

II. The Gospel tells us nothing in detail of the journey of the Holy Family. But it is generally supposed that Mary and her Divine Child rode upon an ass, which was led by Joseph. Perhaps they sometimes lose their way in these unknown mountains, yet never does a word of complaint escape their lips. Joseph walks by the side of the ass, which perhaps besides his tools, carries some of the scanty luggage, but he has very certainly kept for himself a heavy burden, which he carries upon his shoulders. I can remember having seen in the country, poor peasant families going from one place to another, and carrying their few possessions along with them. The father of the family, a heavy wallet on his back, heads the march, and though bending under his burden, is still always in front of the little caravan. When I consider how easily and pleasantly I have always travelled, and compare my comfortable journeys with that of the Holy Family, I am ashamed to think how often I have grumbled, and complained of this and that.

*Resolution.* Oh! how often might I compare, as I now do, the comforts I daily witness with the life Thou didst lead on earth, O my dearest Jesus, and the pleasures of my daily existence with the hardships of Thy childhood! I desire to acquire this salutary habit and make it familiar to me. My heart will thus be able, without effort, to hold sweet and encouraging communings with God.

*Prayer.* Help me, Lord, to sanctify all the little events of my daily life.

## CHAPTER XVII.

### THE FLIGHT INTO EGYPT.—THE DESERT.

Who arose, and took the child and his mother by night, and retired into Egypt.—*St. Matthew ii. 14.*

*Preparatory Prayer.* Accept, I pray Thee, Divine Lord Jesus, the offering which I here make Thee of my whole being.

I. Having considered the sorrow their hasty departure caused to Joseph, the anxiety of our Blessed Lady and the sweet obedience of Jesus, I will now study with great recollectedness all the little details of their journey. I have sometimes seen pictures representing the Holy Family resting in the desert, the Child Jesus surrounded by angels in attitudes of deepest adoration. I will then picture to myself a host of angels adoring Jesus, and hovering around Mary, as she sits by the side of a fountain, under the shade of a spreading tree. She is very weary: for these holy travellers have wandered far, before they could find water, and shelter from the heat of the sun. Mary has not once complained, and when Joseph's anxious glance seems to question her, she endeavours to calm his uneasiness with a gentle smile.

Jesus is in her arms, and in her watchful care for Him she, as it were, forgets herself. With what tender solicitude Joseph on his part endeavours to procure for Mary all that is necessary for Jesus! He clears a space for them under the tree, so that they may have better shelter from the burning rays of the sun. He draws water, lights the fire, and prepares the slender repast: no rest will he take, till all in his power has been done for the precious charge that has been entrusted to him.

II. What a practical lesson for me, and oh! how sadly do I need it! My appearance, my tastes, my wishes, my comforts, in a word, myself, is not this my principal occupation? Oh, when shall I learn to forget myself? When shall I begin to sacrifice myself, for the sake of others, to give pleasure to those around me? Such acts are most acceptable to God. To be entirely occupied with self is very displeasing to Him, and renders one a burden to all.

*Resolution.* I will resolve never to lose an opportunity of giving pleasure to my parents, to my teachers, to my companions, even at the risk of inconvenience to myself; to take the less good place, when there is a question of seeing something; to give up an argument when it can be of no use to any one, and when I see that my opinion hurts or teases; to go out, come in, go hither and thither at the bidding of others, even when it costs me a struggle; and I will do all this with a good grace for God's sake.

*Prayer.* Help my good resolutions, O my God, so that I may have the happiness of always knowing that Thou art pleased with me.

## CHAPTER XVIII.

### ARRIVAL OF THE HOLY FAMILY IN EGYPT.

Who arose, and took the child and his mother by night, and retired into Egypt.—*St. Matt. ii. 14.*

*Preparatory Prayer.* Dear Saviour, permit me to remain at Thy Feet, in the presence of Mary and Joseph, and deign to speak to me Thyself.

I. At last the end of the weary journey draws near. Although the Gospel has given us no details on the subject, I can yet easily imagine the Holy Family arriving in one of the towns of Egypt. The travellers are covered with dust, as they journey along the road that leads to the town. . . . How loudly Joseph's heart must beat, and how troubled must he be, in spite of his outward calm! How will Jesus be received? Where will Mary find a shelter? Joseph is not acquainted with the language of the country. How will he manage to make himself understood? And Mary, surely she too, must feel anxious. She presses to her heart her beloved Jesus—her precious treasure. She does not dare to speak to Joseph of that which is troubling him, for she knows how much he suffers, but in her heart she finds words of peace to console and strengthen him, and he is reassured by her calm confidence.

II. And Jesus? O most dear and Divine Child, make me understand what Thou also dost suffer, though I behold Thee silent and even smiling. Thou dost caress Thy holy Mother and St. Joseph; Thou canst read in the depths of their hearts, so full of sorrow on Thy account. Thou dost suffer for them, but Thou art the Saviour of the world, and Thy suffering becomes an ardent prayer for the salvation of men.

In the contemplation of Jesus, Mary and Joseph, thus sorrowful and anxious for one another, I find a useful lesson for myself. Have I not often seen my parents in grief and sorrow? Family troubles, anxieties about health, faults of character, oh, what numberless causes for sadness in this world! What part have I hitherto played on these occasions? Have I, like Mary and Joseph, sought, by my gentle thoughtfulness, to make my parents forget their grief? Have I ever, like Jesus, prayed for those that suffer?

*Resolution.* When I witness sorrow around me, instead of yielding to ill-humour as I have sometimes done, I will be kind, thoughtful and gentle, and in order that my efforts may be of some use, I will pray with all my heart for those that are in sorrow, and will unite my prayers with those of Jesus, praying for His holy Mother and adopted father, suffering on His account.

*Prayer.* O my God, teach me how strict a duty it

is for me to share the trials and sorrows of my parents; teach me to console them, by praying and suffering with them and for them.

## CHAPTER XIX.

### THE HOLY FAMILY SEEK A SHELTER.

Who arose, and took the child and his mother by night, and retired into Egypt.—*St. Matthew ii. 14.*

*Preparatory Prayer.* My God, I consecrate to Thee all my thoughts and resolutions: inspire and bless them, and make me ever eager in Thy service.

I. I will again consider the three holy travellers: and having seen their entrance into the town where they are to sojourn, I will now follow them with great attention.

Generally, when one goes into an unknown country, one makes sure beforehand of finding there some friends or acquaintances, or if one knows nobody, one is careful to procure introductions. But Joseph, on the contrary, started suddenly and hastily to escape the threatened danger, and so let none know the way they went. I therefore behold the humble and unknown caravan going from door to door. Neither Mary nor Joseph can speak the language of the country, and to make themselves understood, they are obliged to employ signs and gestures, which are often misinterpreted. The Holy Family is once more in the same difficulty as at Bethlehem, when Mary, driven away from every door, was at last compelled to take refuge in a wretched stable.

II. I cannot doubt that the sweet patience of Mary and the calm courage of Joseph remain unaltered. But where at last did they find a shelter? The Gospel does not tell us, but I can fancy that they eventually discovered some modest abode. Doubtless, hosts of angels accompany the Son of God, to do Him honour, but this triumph is hidden. On this occasion, O holy angels, ye are not deputed to reveal the presence of your God, as once your songs of gladness announced His birth to the shepherds at Bethlehem. Mary and Joseph continue to lead the same humble, simple life as before, and no one has reason to suspect that the King of heaven and earth is a guest in the land of Egypt. Since Mary, my dear Mother, and her Divine Son live thus unknown, I will venture to approach them, I who have the happiness of knowing them by faith. Permit me, O Mary, to kneel humbly before thee, and to warm with my kisses the Sacred Feet of the Divine Child Jesus, as at the Crib the ass and the ox warmed Him with their breath. Oh! how happy I am to know that, when I kneel before the tabernacle, I am in the presence of my hidden Jesus, and am welcomed by Him!

*Resolution.* I will resolve from henceforth to imitate Him in shunning praise, and in accepting cheerfully to be forgotten and paid no attention to.

*Prayer.* My God, grant that I may love Thee better every day, serve Thee more faithfully, and pray with greater fervour. Let this be the sole object of my ambition.

## CHAPTER XX.

### THE SOJOURN IN EGYPT.

And he was there until the death of Herod: that it might be fulfilled which the Lord spoke by the prophet, saying: Out of Egypt have I called my son.—*St. Matthew ii. 15.*

*Preparatory Prayer.* I place myself with all recollectedness in Thy presence, O Child Jesus, begging of Thee to obtain for me from Thy Heavenly Father, the grace to follow Thee attentively, so as to know Thee better.

I. The Gospel gives us no details of the time which the Holy Family passed in Egypt, but I can easily imagine the difficulties which St. Joseph must have had to encounter. He must find a living for himself, and for the Divine Child and His Mother. Accustomed to labour all his life, he loses no time in seeking employment, but unknown as he is, and a stranger to the customs of the country, he is unable to undertake any work that would leave him free, and is obliged to resign himself to obey other workmen. What a beautiful lesson of humility, for oh, what thoughts must not have arisen in Joseph's heart! He to whom authority had been given over the Blessed Virgin and the Child

Jesus, thus to be obliged to obey another, and that other perhaps a harsh and brutal master! What repugnance must he have had to overcome, and what energy was necessary to hide his feelings! The thought of all this is inexpressibly painful to the Blessed Virgin, for she suffers in the sufferings of Joseph.

II. Mary wishes to share, in her measure and according to her strength, the humiliation and labours of her holy spouse; she assists him as much as possible and gladly renders him all the little services in her power. No doubt she wins many hearts to him by the very beauty and sweetness of her countenance, whilst her calmness in the state of want and misery to which she is reduced, touch all those who learn to know her; little by little she finds means to lighten Joseph's toil. I picture to myself the joy of the Holy Family when evening comes, and Joseph, more wearied by humiliation than fatigue, returns to the blessed dwelling where Mary's devoted care and Jesus' caresses await him.

*Resolution.* I will seriously seek how to make myself useful. I am too young as yet to render important services, but there are many little things that I can do, little acts of thoughtfulness, of obligingness, kindness, or self-sacrifice.

*Prayer.* My God, teach me how serious a duty it is for me to be kind and considerate to those around me. Impress this truth on my heart, and fix it there more and more firmly, according as I grow older.

## CHAPTER XXI.

### THE RETURN TO GALILEE.

But when Herod was dead, behold an Angel of the Lord appeared in sleep to Joseph in Egypt,

Saying: Arise, and take the child and his mother, and go into the land of Israel: for they are dead that sought the life of the child.

Who arose, and took the child and his mother, and came into the land of Israel.

But hearing that Archelaus reigned in Judea in the room of Herod his father, he was afraid to go thither ; and being warned in sleep, retired into the quarters of Galilee.—*St. Matthew ii. 19 to 22.*

*Preparatory Prayer.* Grant me, my God, a sincere desire to know Thee and love Thee as Thou deservest.

I. Little by little the condition of the Holy Family in Egypt improves; Joseph's earnings enable him no doubt to find a more comfortable dwelling-place for Mary. But the Gospel tells us, without revealing the exact time, that Joseph was informed of Herod's death by an angel, who told him to take Jesus back to the land of Israel. O Joseph, art thou not at last tempted to complain ? For this journey will be still more fatiguing than the first. The Child Jesus has grown, and Mary will consequently have a heavier weight to carry; Jesus Himself will suffer more, and work and the means of living will again be wanting.

No matter, Joseph obeys without raising the slightest objection.

II. He makes his preparations quietly, for this time no danger obliges them to depart in haste. But a new trial was in store. Their departure gave rise to more than one comment from their neighbours, who no doubt overwhelmed them with questions; for to those who knew not Who Jesus was, and who were ignorant of the reasons that had rendered it necessary for Him to hide Himself in Egypt, and of God's command to take Him back again, these long journeys, undertaken by people obliged to earn their bread, seemed foolish and uncalled for. Joseph no doubt suffered deeply, but his lips were sealed.

The women of the neighbourhood came to Mary to question her, and weary her with their arguments and reproaches. But she, always kind and gentle, suffered their importunity with patience, treasuring her precious secret in the depths of her heart. These very importunities should make me understand how wrong it is to be always minding other people's business, making rash judgments, finding fault with, or asking questions about what does not concern me. How often would not a decision, which seems absurd, appear most reasonable did we but know the real cause for it.

*Resolution.* I will no longer busy myself about other

people's affairs; I will ask no indiscreet questions, nor be so ready to give my own opinion.

*Prayer.* My God, make me understand, I entreat, how displeasing to Thee is idle curiosity, so that I may carefully avoid it, and never lose time, every moment of which is so precious.

## CHAPTER XXII.

### THE ARRIVAL AT NAZARETH.

And coming he dwelt in a city called Nazareth: that it might be fulfilled which was said by the prophets: That he shall be called a Nazarite.—*St. Matthew ii. 23.*

*Preparatory Prayer.* Lord, teach me to be truly recollected in Thy presence, so that I may learn to reflect, to meditate and to pray.

I. I will follow Jesus, Mary and Joseph on their journey, as I once followed their flight into Egypt. I will again watch them as they halt from time to time, and compassionate their sufferings from thirst, and from the burning heat of the sun. I will contemplate the angels accompanying the holy travellers and watching tenderly over Jesus, and will picture to myself the Divine Infant, sleeping on the knees of the Blessed Virgin, whilst Joseph prepares all that is needful for the Mother and Child. At Thy Feet, O Jesus, I now ask myself whither did the Holy Family direct their steps on quitting Egypt? The Gospel tells us how the Angel made known to Joseph that he might return into the land of Israel, without specially naming the town to which he was to go; but St. Matthew adds that Joseph went to dwell in Nazareth, and that thus were accomplished these words of the prophet concerning Jesus: "He shall be called a Nazarite."

II. Before proceeding further, I desire to thank Thee, O my God, for this miraculous accord between the prophecies and the events of our Saviour's life on earth; to-day this instance strikes me and forces me to reflect; but were I better instructed, and had I the desire to understand more fully the admirable ways of Divine Providence, what a number of examples should I not find in the Holy Scriptures! How beautifully have not all the prophecies concerning our Lord been fulfilled! O my God, how great and grand is all Thou dost! Oh! how can understandings so poor so limited as ours, sometimes doubt Thy all-powerful wisdom!

My God, I thank Thee for having bestowed on me the gift of faith, and for having placed me under the care of Christian parents or superiors, who have taught me to know Thee.

*Resolution.* I will consider attentively how the smallest events are directed by Almighty God, even as were the prophecies concerning Jesus. I will often make acts of faith in the Providence of God.

*Prayer.* Teach me, O my God, to offer Thee all the events of my life, and always to consecrate to Thee all my actions, my efforts and my desires.

## CHAPTER XXIII.

### THE HOLY FAMILY AT NAZARETH.

And the child grew, and waxed strong, full of wisdom: and the grace of God was in him.—*St. Luke ii. 40.*

*Preparatory Prayer.* Behold me in Thy presence, O Divine Jesus; bless me and deign to accept the offering I make Thee of my thoughts and resolutions.

I. Let us enter Nazareth with the Holy Family. Joseph has at last reached the end of his journey; he is no doubt glad to find himself again in his own country; but his thoughts are more occupied with Jesus and Mary than with himself, and he thanks God for having protected them in the midst of the dangers they encountered, whilst obeying His command.

As to the most Blessed Virgin, she had formerly quitted her home and her family without a murmur; I remember how promptly she obeyed when Joseph told her of God's command that they should fly into Egypt.

Although the Gospel, in relating this circumstance, does not make any comment upon it, I can yet easily understand how cruelly the tender loving heart of Mary must have suffered, when bidding adieu to her relatives, and leaving her humble but happy home.

II. If I, whose heart is so cold, when compared to our Lady's, am grieved at being separated for a short time from my father or mother; if leaving home seems to me a hard trial, how much then must not Mary have suffered! As the little caravan approaches Nazareth, how loudly, therefore, must her heart beat, divided as it is between the joy of coming back, and the fear of no longer finding those whom she had left behind. In those days communication was rare and difficult, and probably Mary and Joseph had had no news of their friends during their absence. Whom then will they find, and of whom will death have deprived them? These thoughts fill their minds as they approach their former abode.

And Jesus? Although He seems but an ordinary Child, without experience of the sorrows and anxieties of life, He reads in the hearts of His Mother and St. Joseph, and therefore looks upon them with redoubled tenderness; He caresses Mary, embraces her and leans His little Head upon her shoulder.

*Resolution.* I will endeavour to acquire a habit of making frequent acts of confidence in God, and will ask of Him alone all that is needful for my parents.

*Prayer.* O Jesus, my Saviour, grant that this meditation may bear fruit in my soul; teach me to draw from it an increase of love for Thee, a tender devotion to Mary, a child-like confidence in Joseph, and a complete acquiescence in Thy Divine Providence.

## CHAPTER XXIV.

### THE HIDDEN LIFE AT NAZARETH.

And he went down with them, and came to Nazareth: **and was subject to them.**—*St. Luke ii. 51.*

*Preparatory Prayer.* I wish to contemplate Thee, Divine Lord, in Thy humble dwelling at Nazareth. Permit me to enter that blessed abode, and make me understand its hidden grandeur.

I. Without knowing the exact age of the Child Jesus, when He returned from Egypt, for this the Gospel does not tell us, the date of Herod's death leads us to the conclusion, that He must have been between four and seven years old. He was therefore quite a little Child, and incapable of any fatiguing work. Nevertheless, when I remember all that is done in the peasant or artizan class, by even the youngest child to help its mother in household work, I can imagine what a number of useful things the Child Jesus must have found to do. I will then try to picture Him to myself, at times going to draw water at the nearest well, at others carrying sticks, and seeing to the fire, or helping to prepare the humble meals. Sometimes He goes into Joseph's workshop, and there, although His tiny Hands are not strong enough to work, He seeks every opportunity of assisting His foster-father, giving him his tools, or picking up the shavings. When Joseph has at last finished his hard day's toil, the Divine Child, anxious to spare him all further fatigue, carefully sweeps out the workshop, and puts everything in its place.

II. So much for His outward acts; but who can tell what respectful tenderness my Saviour shews towards His parents, while fulfilling these humble duties? With what sweet seriousness and serenity He addresses them: how full of deference and affection is His manner, and how loving the expression of His Divine Countenance, when, in the midst of His occupations, He pauses to imprint a kiss on Mary's forehead, or seating Himself beside Joseph, makes him by His tender words forget his weariness! O my good Jesus, what a beautiful example, and what reflections it suggests to my mind!

Alas! how humbled should I be, when I consider my conduct towards my parents!

*Resolution.* Dear Lord, I firmly resolve to endeavour, from this day forward, to imitate Thy gentleness, Thy tenderness towards Thy parents, and the ready industry with which Thou didst serve them on so many occasions.

*Prayer.* O Jesus, Who didst constitute the happiness of Mary and Joseph, grant me the grace to be, like Thee, the happiness of my parents.

## CHAPTER XXV.

### JESUS IS TAKEN TO JERUSALEM FOR THE PASCH.

And his parents went every year to Jerusalem, at the solemn day of the pasch.

And when he was twelve years old, they going up into Jerusalem according to the custom of the feast. . . . .—*St. Luke ii. 41 and 42.*

*Preparatory Prayer.* My God, do Thou Thyself so speak to my heart, that it may love Thee better.

I. The Holy Family dwelt in Nazareth, and only quitted it on certain days, in order to fulfil the law of God: and for this purpose they went every year to Jerusalem to keep the feast of the Pasch. All the people of the country, that were able, went there, and very often together, and thus the inhabitants of the different villages or the members of a large family travelled in company. So too in our own times, do we see, on certain great feasts, numbers of people going together to visit some holy shrine. Every year then Joseph took Jesus and Mary to Jerusalem.

II. Their travelling companions, although they little knew how favoured they were, in thus being in the company of the Son of God, must nevertheless have felt singularly drawn towards Jesus. I can fancy how the little children instinctively gathered around Him, listening to His words, and following His example in everything. Unconsciously to themselves, their hearts were touched, the kindness of Jesus won them all, for the Son of the Most High, laying aside His grandeur to make Himself like them, was in their eyes an ordinary child, taking part in, and seeming to enjoy their games, and sharing their little troubles as well as their pleasures.

Here will I pause, O my God. What a lesson for me! How much I need to learn from the Child Jesus how I should act towards my brothers and sisters, my friends and companions? Am I kind, thoughtful, amiable and gentle towards them? Do I try to console them in their troubles? Do I, in order to give them pleasure, lay aside my own wishes, and consent to such and such a game, when I would like another better myself? Or if I do consent, is it not with an air of vexation and annoyance?

*Resolution.* I will to-day generously perform all the little acts of kindness that may come in my way.

*Prayer.* O sweet benevolence of the Child Jesus, take possession of my heart, and make me like my Divine Model.

---

## CHAPTER XXVI.

### THE HOLY FAMILY AT JERUSALEM.

And his parents went every year to Jerusalem, at the solemn day of the pasch.

And when he was twelve years old, they going up into Jerusalem according to the custom of the feast. . . . .—*St. Luke ii. 41, 42.*

*Preparatory Prayer.* O Jesus, my Saviour, be with me, I pray Thee, and make me attentive to Thy Divine lessons.

I. I have already seen how the Holy Family went every year to Jerusalem. I now wish to accompany them to the Temple, remaining close to the Child Jesus. I will therefore follow Mary, Joseph and the Divine Child. How full of gravity and at the same time of serenity, are their three countenances telling so plainly of peace with God! Jesus is profoundly recollected, and the sweet expression of His Face seems to invite one to pray with Him. He does not hurry, but proceeds in silence: it is easy to guess that His Heart is raised on high, and that He converses silently with His Heavenly Father. He is surrounded by a crowd of grown-up persons and children, who do not know Him. They are going to the Temple to assist at the Sacrifices about to be offered there. He offers Himself to His Father for the ransom of all; He sees beforehand His sufferings, His anguish, and His labours; He knows the ingratitude of men and their deplorable blindness, and He accepts it all.

II. Thus does He enter the Temple, and place Himself obediently, where Joseph tells Him, by Mary's side, and His Heart renews and continues the offering of His Life for all mankind. He is there in the midst of the crowd, lost in its vast multitude: but God looks upon Him, this Divine Child, Whom one day He will designate by these words pronounced from on high: "This is my beloved Son." God then listens to His prayer, and looks upon Him with complacency.

*Resolution.* Although I am but a child, I know that God listens to my prayers, provided they are united with that of Jesus. I therefore resolve to say all mine as though I were repeating them with the Divine Child, so that God may look upon and listen to me.

*Prayer.* Vouchsafe, I beg of Thee, O my God, to increase my piety, so that my prayers may be agreeable in Thy sight, and that Thou mayest deign to accept them.

## CHAPTER XXVII.

### JESUS IS LOST BY HIS PARENTS.

And having fulfilled the days, when they returned, the child Jesus remained in Jerusalem, and his parents knew it not.

And thinking that he was in the company, they came a day's journey, and sought him among their kinsfolk and acquaintance.—*St. Luke ii. 43, 44.*

*Preparatory Prayer.* Holy Virgin, my tender Mother, I place myself this day under thy protection, obtain for me the light of the Holy Spirit. I consecrate all my thoughts to thy Divine Son.

I. When the Child Jesus was twelve years old, He came to Jerusalem, as He was accustomed to do every year. After the feast, His parents set out on their return to Nazareth, without perceiving that He had remained behind: they thought He was in the company of some of their friends or kinsfolk. I cannot doubt how much it cost Mary not to have Jesus with her on the way, for she must have suffered greatly, every time that she was separated from her Divine Child. But most certainly she considered all the good, those who approached her Son, received from the Words of Life that fell from His Lips, and this Blessed Mother was too well accustomed to forget herself, for the glory of God and the good of others, to allow this opportunity for self-sacrifice to escape her.

II. On arriving, however, at the end of the first day's journey, Mary and Joseph begin to be uneasy at not seeing Jesus, Who, always full of deference and tenderness towards them, is never long out of their presence.

In their anxiety, they go hither and thither, from group to group, in search of their Divine Son, questioning all whom they meet. Mary, her eyes filled with tears, and her countenance expressing the deepest anguish, is nevertheless calm, and in the midst of her search, constantly raises her heart to God, begging of Him to have pity upon her. Joseph, too, is deeply afflicted, and asks himself, if he is not to blame for having lost the Divine Child. He humbles himself, and begs pardon of God for having perchance failed to watch carefully enough over the Sacred Charge that had been confided to him. Everyone pities them, and yet none can tell the anguish of their hearts. They alone, indeed, know the supreme treasure that they have lost,—Jesus, the Son of God, the Author of Grace, the Light and the Life.

*Resolution.* I will watch carefully over my mind and my heart, in order not to lose the grace of God and the love of Jesus.

*Prayer.* O my Saviour, may this picture of the sufferings of Thy beloved parents, make me understand how great a misfortune it is to lose Thee. Preserve me, all my life, from so great an evil, and teach me from henceforth to pray for all poor sinners who have lost Thy grace.

## CHAPTER XXVIII.

### MARY AND JOSEPH AT JERUSALEM.

And not finding him, they returned into Jerusalem, seeking him.—*St. Luke ii. 45.*

*Preparatory Prayer.* My God, grant that I may be truly recollected, so that I may profit by these moments of prayer.

I. After having sought Jesus amongst their relations and friends, St. Joseph and the Blessed Virgin do not hesitate to return even to Jerusalem, as the Gospel tells us. Oh! how sadly they retrace the path, so lately trod with Jesus! How anxiously they look out for Him all the way, constantly hoping to meet their dear Son! They interrogate the passers by, and Mary enters many a house to ask if her Son has not been seen. I can better understand the Blessed Virgin's sorrow, by calling to mind my mother's grief, when she is separated from one of my brothers or sisters, or when she does not receive any news of them: how anxious she then is! And Mary loved Jesus better than any mother loves her children, for this Child was her God.

II. Mary and Joseph continue on their way without success, and arrive at last at Jerusalem. But what can they do there? How can they hope to find Jesus in that immense city? Still, they know many people, and they inquire every where; but alas! their search is in vain: no one has seen Him. Some to whom they go are full of compassion, and seek to comfort them in their sorrow. Others, on the contrary, express astonishment; and perhaps Mary and Joseph have to listen to hard and unjust remarks about their want of care and the undutifulness of Jesus in leaving them. Silence, gentleness and resignation are their only answers.

*Resolution.* When I receive some rebuke, either merited or not, I will be silent, remembering the humility of Mary.

*Prayer.* O Mary, O Joseph, teach me to act like you, and if ever I receive unmerited reproaches, obtain for me the grace to offer up to God the pain they cause me, and grant that I may speak of them to Him alone.

## CHAPTER XXIX.

### THE FINDING OF JESUS IN THE TEMPLE.

And it came to pass, that after three days they found him in the temple sitting in the midst of the doctors, hearing them and asking them questions.

And all that heard him were astonished at his wisdom and his answers.

And seeing him, they wondered. And his mother said to him: Son, why hast thou done so to us? behold thy father and I have sought thee sorrowing.

And he said to them: How is it that you sought me? did you not know that I must be about my Father's business?

And they understood not the word that he spoke unto them.
—*St. Luke ii. 46 to 50.*

*Preparatory Prayer.* O Lord, hear my prayer, and do Thou deign to rule over all my thoughts, desires and resolutions.

I. After three long days of search, Jesus' parents at last find Him in the Temple. I have followed them in spirit during these three days, and now also accompany them as they ascend the steps of the sacred edifice.— They pass under its massive columns, and anxiously tread their way through its numerous passages. At last they reach that part of the building where the doctors of the law are in the habit of assembling, in order to study the Holy Scriptures. Oh, what a joyful surprise, what unspeakable happiness! Jesus is in the midst of the doctors. . . . It is indeed Himself, standing there, clothed in the humble garb of a poor child! His calm beautiful Countenance, so young and yet so grave, is in striking contrast with the withered faces and snowy locks of the greater number of doctors, who listen to Him full of wonder and admiration. His child-like voice speaks with unwonted authority.

II. But Mary, without hesitation, enters the venerable group, and clasping Jesus to her heart, tenderly reproaches Him in these words, which the Gospel has handed down to us: "Son, why hast thou done so to us? behold thy father and I have sought thee sorrowing."—*And he said to them:* "How is it that you sought me? did you not know that I must be about my Father's business."

No doubt, in the midst of their joy at finding Him again, this answer must have caused them pain; but they knew that the words of Jesus were the words of God Himself: and though, as the Gospel tells us, they understood not the word that He spoke unto them, yet their faith and docility to the Holy Ghost were such, that they sought not to comprehend this strange behaviour on the part of Jesus, generally so submissive. And, adds the Gospel, "his mother kept all these words in her heart." It is then by meditating on the words of our Lord, that is to say, keeping them in my heart and often dwelling upon them, that I shall learn that union with God which helps us to bear everything, to accept everything, and to bless Divine Providence in all times and places: in this consists true happiness.

*Resolution.* Every day I will select a special passage in my meditation, and I will endeavour to call it to mind several times during the day.

*Prayer.* O Mary, my beloved Mother, teach me how to meditate like thee, and to keep in my heart the pious thoughts with which the Holy Ghost inspires me.

## CHAPTER XXX.

### JESUS' HIDDEN LIFE AT NAZARETH.

And he went down with them, and came to Nazareth : and was subject to them. And his mother kept all these words in her heart.

And Jesus advanced in wisdom and age, and grace with God and men.—*St. Luke ii. 51, 52.*

*Preparatory Prayer.* Behold me prostrate at Thy Feet, O my dear Master, do not refuse me Thy holy grace.

I. Jesus, having quitted Jerusalem with His parents, went down into Nazareth, and was subject to them. These three lines comprehend all our Saviour's life till He was thirty years of age. I desire now to study with reverence the years that followed Jesus' return to Nazareth, after His parents had found Him in the Temple.

He is not yet old enough to assist Joseph materially in his work. But having seen how useful He made Himself, even when quite a little child, to Mary in her household cares, and to Joseph in the countless little services he needed in his workshop, I can easily picture Him to myself beginning to learn the trade of a carpenter. I can imagine Him, obedient and attentive to all that Joseph tells Him, engrossed in His work, this Divine Apprentice, listening to His master's teaching. What a beautiful sight for angels to gaze upon! Their Sovereign Lord, the Master of all science, humbling Himself, even if one may dare to say it, to the awkwardness of a little apprentice of twelve years old!

II. Dear Jesus, tell me why Thou, Who knowest all things, dost choose to appear ignorant of everything? Why give Thyself so much trouble to handle the plane, Thou Who didst create both heaven and earth? I see Thee, weary with Thy efforts, beginning again and again; bringing Thy little attempts to Joseph, and, at a word from him, commencing anew. Thy little Hands, unaccustomed to hard work, are swollen, sometimes even bleeding. Ah! why not succeed at the first attempt? I seem to hear Thee reply: *It is for thee, my child*, that I act thus, to teach thee how to work, to take trouble, to accept the fatigue and weariness that always accompany the efforts one must make, in order to learn anything. For, whether it be manual labour or study, we must all have our share of work, of effort, and fatigue. I thank Thee, Lord Jesus, for having given me this beautiful example.

*Resolution.* When I have to exert myself, when I find work difficult and laborious, I will remember how Jesus laboured and toiled, and will therefore apply myself courageously to my task.

*Prayer.* Divine Carpenter of Nazareth, may the remembrance of the labours of Thy youth come to my mind, whenever I feel discouraged and disinclined to work. I promise Thee this day to endeavour most earnestly to please Thee.

## CHAPTER XXXI.

### JESUS WORKS AS A CARPENTER.

Is not this the carpenter's son ? Is not his mother called Mary ?—*St. Matthew xiii. 55.*

*Preparatory Prayer.* Penetrate my heart, I beseech Thee, O Lord, with a true love of Thee, so that all my thoughts may turn to Thee alone.

I. The Divine Apprentice, Whom I have seen, as a child, learning Joseph's trade, Himself becomes, by degrees, a skilful workman.

Full of health, of courage, and of affection for His parents, He it is Who now supports the Holy Family by His toil. Joseph has grown old and feeble ; Jesus therefore takes upon Himself all the difficult and laborious work, leaving only to his adopted father such little occupations, as serve to distract, without fatiguing him.

A pious tradition tells us that Joseph made ploughs. It was then in making ploughs that our Saviour must have passed the first fifteen years of His life. Oh, what a touching sight I behold in this poor carpenter's workshop ! Mary, my dearest Mother, permit me, I pray thee, to enter : let me station myself close to thee, so that I may hear and see all that is taking place.

II. I will then place myself at the feet of the

Blessed Virgin, who is busy with her work, and from time to time raises her eyes to gaze upon her beloved Son. She keeps in her heart the slightest words that fall from His Lips. Jesus stands by His table, at times occupied in fashioning the timber, at others collecting together the large heavy pieces of wood, and sparing neither fatigue nor trouble to make His work as perfect as possible. I see Him resting from time to time; He has need of repose, this dear Saviour, for He suffers like other men, and labour is as fatiguing to Him as to them. He often addresses His holy Mother and St. Joseph, explaining to them certain passages in Holy Scripture; He foretells the sufferings that await Him, and constantly raises their hearts above this world, while His beautiful Countenance beams with a celestial light.

He then resumes His laborious work, and though His Lips are closed, who can tell the sublime communings of His Heart with His Heavenly Father? O my Jesus, what lessons for myself I find in the study I have just made of Thy hidden life at Nazareth! Humility, union with God, self-sacrifice and prayer.

*Resolution.* I will try, in future, to be always polite and considerate to the labouring classes.

*Prayer.* Thou dost teach me, O Jesus, by Thy patient toil, the respect I should have for work, for Thou didst choose the humble condition of a poor workman. Never let me be tempted to despise those who gain their livelihood in the same manner.

# CHAPTER XXXII.

## JESUS LEAVES NAZARETH.

And it came to pass: in those days Jesus came from Nazareth of Galilee: and was baptised by John in the Jordan.—*St. Mark* i. 9.

*Preparatory Prayer.* O my dear Saviour, deign to speak to me Thyself, and inspire me with the thoughts and resolutions most pleasing to Thee.

I. Jesus Christ was thirty years of age when He commenced His public life. The Gospel gives us no exact details concerning the Holy Family during the years that followed Jesus' return to Nazareth, when He was twelve years old. 'He was subject to them:' these are the only words that reveal to us in some sort that hidden life whose sublime lessons we have endeavoured to understand. At last the solemn moment approaches when our Lord is about to manifest Himself to the world. The time has come for Him to quit His humble home at Nazareth; He must bid farewell to Mary. The Blessed Virgin has long prepared herself for this cruel separation. I can fancy how Jesus must have redoubled His respectful tenderness towards His holy Mother, as the day of sacrifice draws near.

II. Oh! what a trial for Mary! True she has had, since the birth of her Son, many moments of bitter anguish, and the sword of sorrow, foretold by Simeon, has never ceased to pierce her heart. She has often pondered upon the sufferings she knew were in store. . . . . But now the moment has come when, for her, the first part of the sacrifice begins. Jesus no doubt told her, the preceding evening, that it would be the last passed together. Oh! how Mary must have felt her courage fail with the first dawn of that day that was to separate her from her beloved Son! But she raises her heart to God, and is calm and resigned, even now, at the moment of parting.

Jesus stands by her side, and speaks to her of His Heavenly Father, of the Divine mission He is about to accomplish,—the salvation of mankind,—and Mary's heart accepts all, and offers all to God in union with the sacrifice of Jesus. Having clasped her dear Son to her heart, she humbly kneels at His Feet and receives His Divine blessing.

O Mary, when thou dost arise, Jesus is gone, thou art alone, for tradition tells us that Joseph was then no more. Alone! Oh! what a void, what sadness in the little home once so happy! It is to save mankind, it is to save *me*, that Jesus leaves Mary thus alone. I will then shew great respect and love to this dear Mother.

*Resolution.* When God demands of me some separation, some little sacrifice, that costs my heart a pang,

I will not murmur, but will think of the separation of Jesus and Mary.

*Prayer.* Deign, O Mary, to receive me, accept the offering of my filial devotion, notwithstanding my weakness. I love thee with all my heart and desire to share thy sorrow. Oh, make me always thy most loving and obedient child!

## CHAPTER XXXIII.

### THE BAPTISM OF JESUS CHRIST.

Now it came to pass when all the people were baptized, that Jesus also being baptized and praying, heaven was opened: And the Holy Ghost descended in a bodily shape as a dove upon him: and a voice came from heaven: Thou art my beloved Son, in thee I am well pleased.—*St. Luke iii 21, 22.*

*Preparatory Prayer.* I desire, O my Jesus, to be very recollected in Thy holy presence. Help me, by Thy grace, and make me understand Thy adorable life.

I. Immediately after quitting Nazareth, our Lord goes in search of Saint John the Baptist, on the banks of the Jordan, and, entering the river, is baptised. The Holy Ghost descends upon Him in the form of a dove, and a voice from Heaven is heard to say: "Thou art My beloved Son, in Thee I am well pleased."

I can imagine the admiration of Saint John, the astonishment of the crowd, and the profound recollectedness of Jesus. Since the night of His birth, when angels had announced the joyful tidings, Heaven had been silent. For thirty years His Heavenly Father had left Him to struggle all alone against every difficulty, without revealing His Divinity. But now before He commences His public life, His life of suffering and toil for souls, His Father on high wishes to make known to the world the Divinity of His beloved Son.

And yet, O my dear Saviour, I see Thee, still as simple and as poor as before. After this solemn manifestation, Thou dost direct Thy steps towards the desert, there to fast for forty days and forty nights, dividing Thy time between prayer and penance.

II. I notice that the baptism, administered by John, was not the same that was later instituted by Jesus Christ. The former was only a baptism of penance. How striking is the circumstance that our Lord's two first acts, on quitting Nazareth, were acts of penance. From this I should learn that penance is indispensable. I must not imagine that it is only meant for saints or religious; penance must be practised by all; I myself must practise it.

*Resolution.* I will, like Jesus Christ, faithfully answer God's call, and will not let a day pass without finding at least one little opportunity of mortifying myself, whether it be in depriving myself at table of some little delicacy, refraining from asking an unnecessary question, or doing something I dislike rather than something else that pleases me. I will courageously perform all these little acts of penance, suitable to my age, remembering that, small as they are, they are very pleasing to God.

*Prayer.* Lord Jesus, make me truly understand the necessity of doing penance, so that I may acquire the habit of frequently making little acts of mortification.

# CHAPTER XXXIV.

## THE MARRIAGE FEAST AT CANA.

There was a marriage in Cana of Galilee: and the mother of Jesus was there.
And Jesus also was invited, and his disciples to the marriage.
—*St. John ii. 1, 2.*

*Preparatory Prayer.* Fill my heart, O God, with love of Thee; deign to inspire me with holy thoughts and good resolutions.

I. On leaving the desert, our Lord rejoined Saint John on the banks of the Jordan, and afterwards returned to Galilee to His holy Mother. It was then that He was invited with her to a marriage feast in Cana, where His first miracle was to take place. I can easily imagine Mary's joy, when Jesus returned, and when He told her that He would accompany her to Cana. The absence of her Divine Son must have been unspeakably painful to the Blessed Virgin. Prayer and submission to the Will of God had however sustained her. What a lesson for me, did I but know how to profit by it! Instead of tears and lamentations, when separated from those I love, I will seek strength from God, and will henceforth try to remember that a sacrifice offered to Him loses half its bitterness.

II. I behold Jesus and Mary setting out on their way to, and arriving at the house of the friends, who have invited them to be present at the feast. I can imagine how busy everyone must have been, for the guests are numerous, and are placed according to their rank. Mary is not far from her Son, and whilst graciously answering those who address her, she often looks at her beloved Jesus, renewing at every glance her love and devotion. As at all numerous assemblies, there are persons who, carried away by excitement, abandon themselves to excessive gaiety. The calm and beautiful Countenance of Jesus is in striking contrast with their levity. How self-possessed He is, and yet how kind and affable to those around Him !

*Resolution.* O Jesus, Thy presence at the marriage feast at Cana, is a great example for me. I learn from it how I should comport myself at the little family gatherings at which I sometimes assist. What have I hitherto done on such occasions ? Have I not often, yielding to the excitement of pleasure, laughed and talked immoderately, little caring how I annoyed and fatigued other people ? As I desire that this shall no longer be the case, I will often ask myself when I am in society : " What would Jesus have said ; what would He have done, if circumstanced as I am ? "

*Prayer.* My God, help me by Thy holy Grace, to be faithful to my resolution, and make me always and everywhere worthy to be looked upon and loved by Thee.

# CHAPTER XXXV.

## THE WATER CHANGED TO WINE.

And the wine failing, the mother of Jesus saith to him: They have no wine.

And Jesus saith to her: Woman, what is it to me, and to thee? My hour is not yet come.

His mother saith to the waiters: Whatsoever he shall say to you, do ye.

Now there were set there six water-pots of stone, according to the manner of the purifying of the Jews, containing two or three measures a piece.

Jesus saith to them: Fill the water-pots with water. And they filled them up to the brim.

And Jesus saith to them: Draw out now, and carry to the chief steward of the feast. And they carried it.

And when the chief steward had tasted the water made wine, and knew not whence it was, but the waiters knew who had drawn the water: the chief steward calleth the bridegroom,

And saith to him: Every man at first setteth forth good wine: and when men have well drank, then that which is worse: but thou hast kept the good wine until now.—*St. John ii. 3-10.*

*Preparatory Prayer.* Behold me, O God, in Thy holy presence: I desire to study the miracle of the water changed to wine; do Thou Thyself direct all my thoughts and affections.

I. I have already remarked the striking contrast between the calm gravity of Jesus, and the levity of those around Him. I now desire to watch with increasing attention what is about to take place. The servants and attendants run anxiously hither and thither, and whisper to the master of the house: "there is no more wine." The guests have not the slightest idea of this, and continue to drink what they have, or to ask for more. The host's uneasiness does not escape Mary, who is ever ready to share the troubles, great or small, of her fellow-creatures. Turning to Jesus, she whispers in His ear: "They have no wine:" then, calling to her side one of the attendants, she says to him: "Whatsoever He shall say to you, do ye."

II. The attendants approach Jesus, without at all understanding how He can help them, but they obey. Now there were there six stone jars, and Jesus told them to fill them with water.

Docile to His voice, they hasten to execute His command. "Draw out now," adds our Lord, when the jars were filled with water. How great must be their surprise, when they find the water changed into excellent wine. This was my Saviour's first miracle. He wished to work it at the request of His beloved Mother, and in order to render a service of simple kindness.

I find two lessons in this miracle, as related in Holy Writ. First, it is to Mary that we should make known our wants, begging of her to present our prayers to her Divine Son, for this is the surest means of obtaining what we need. Secondly, we should not confine ourselves to asking for great graces, but should, with a child-like confidence in Jesus and Mary, have recourse to them in all the circumstances of our lives.

*Resolution.* I will always place myself in spirit close to the Blessed Virgin, and when I am anxious or in trouble, or when inspired by a holy desire, I will turn towards her, telling her, with great simplicity, all that is passing in my mind.

*Prayer.* O Mary, my tender Mother, deign I beg of thee, to present all my needs to thy Divine Son. As thou didst whisper to Him at the feast at Cana: 'They have no wine,' say to Him to-day: 'This child is sorely in need of such a virtue,' and now, as then, O Mary, thy prayer will be heard.

## CHAPTER XXXVI.

### THE CALL OF THE APOSTLES.

And Jesus walking by the sea of Galilee, saw two brethren, Simon who is called Peter, and Andrew his brother, casting a net into the sea (for they were fishers).

And he saith to them: Come ye after me, and I will make you to be fishers of men.

And they immediately leaving their nets, followed him.

And going on from thence, he saw other two brethren, James the son of Zebedee, and John his brother, in a ship with Zebedee their father, mending their nets: and he called them.

And they forthwith left their nets and father and followed him.—*St. Matthew iv. 18-22.*

*Preparatory Prayer.* Divine Master, teach me, I implore, to know, to love and to imitate Thee.

I. The Gospel tells us that Jesus, after leaving Cana, went to Capharnaum. Our Lord often dwelt there during the years of His public life, although from the day when he quitted Nazareth, He had never any fixed abode, but wandered unceasingly through Judea, Samaria and Galilee, teaching the people, visiting the small towns, stopping sometimes in one country, sometimes in another, and publishing everywhere the joyful tidings. How often in His journeys, this good Master must have been repulsed, fatigued, overcome by heat, and sometimes even by hunger!

II. One day, quite in the beginning of His Apostolic life, "Jesus walking by the Sea of Galilee, saw two brethren, Simon who is called Peter, and Andrew his brother, casting a net into the sea (for they were fishers). And He saith to them: *Come ye after Me, and I will make you to be fishers of men.* And they immediately leaving their nets, followed Him. And going on from thence, He saw other two brethren, James the son of Zebedee, and John his brother, in a ship with Zebedee their father, mending their nets: and He called them. And they forthwith left their nets and father and followed Him."

This is how the holy Gospel relates the call of the first Apostles. I will henceforth picture Jesus to myself, surrounded by His disciples. I see this gentle Saviour drawing to Himself these rough men, by the sweetness of His Countenance, and still more by His Divine influence. O Jesus, Who didst say to Simon and Andrew, 'Come ye after Me,' hast Thou ever ceased during the last eighteen hundred years to repeat these same words? Is it not thus that Thou speakest to my heart, every time Thou dost inspire it with some good resolution? My child, follow Me, that is to say, do not resist My grace, listen to My voice, and draw near to Me, that thou mayest gain strength faithfully to accomplish the duties of thy age and state.

*Resolution.* Whenever I hear the voice of God, I

will respond as promptly to His call, as did the disciples, in other words I will do, well and quickly, all that Almighty God asks of me.

*Prayer.* O Jesus, whilst Thy Divine words fall upon our ears, Thy grace falls upon our hearts: grant that I may be always obedient to Thy voice, and faithful to Thy grace.

# CHAPTER XXXVII.

## JESUS IN THE BARK OF SIMON.

And going up into one of the ships that was Simon's, he desired him to draw back a little from the land. And sitting he taught the multitudes out of the ship.

Now when he had ceased to speak, he said to Simon: Launch out into the deep, and let down your nets for a draught.

And Simon answering, said to him: Master we have laboured all the night, and have taken nothing: but at thy word I will let down the net.

And when they had done this, they enclosed a very great multitude of fishes, and their net broke.

And they beckoned to their partners that were in the other ship, that they should come and help them. And they came, and filled both the ships, so that they were almost sinking.

Which when Simon Peter saw, he fell down at Jesus' knees, saying: Depart from me, for I am a sinful man, O Lord.

For he was wholly astonished, and all that were with him, at the draught of the fishes which they had taken.—*St. Luke v. 3-9.*

*Preparatory Prayer.* Bless me, I beg of Thee, O my God, and deign to inspire me with holy thoughts, whilst I study the adorable life of Thy Son Jesus.

I. One day that He was on the shore of the Lake of

Genesareth, our Lord was surrounded by a great crowd who came to hear Him. These people were eager to receive the teachings of our Saviour, for those that had already heard Him, spoke to others of His preaching, and the multitude imperceptibly increased. Our dear Lord, no matter how much He needed repose, always forgot His own weariness, and never refused to the people the lessons they had come to hear.

That day, seeing two boats, He entered one of them, which belonged to Simon, and told the latter to draw back a little from the land. He then preached thence to the crowd, and having finished His discourse, told Simon to launch out into the deep, and to cast his nets. The fisherman had laboured in vain all night, and was weary with fruitless toil. Nevertheless, he at once says to Jesus: "Master, at Thy word I will let down the net." His obedience, and blind faith in the words of Jesus, will most certainly be blessed.

II. Indeed the net becomes at once so full that the meshes break, and Saint Peter is obliged to call his companions to his assistance. The boats are so laden that they are in great danger of sinking. Peter and his comrades are terrified, but Jesus reassures them; and the Gospel adds, that having brought their boats back to the shore, they quitted all and followed our Lord.

*Resolution.* I too, like Peter and his companions, am often frightened by difficulties, and wearied by the apparent failure of long and tiresome work. I will, in future, obey as promptly as St. Peter, cost what it may, in all that I know to be the Will of God.

*Prayer.* May the example of Thy apostles, O my God, increase my faith, my love and my fidelity in following Thee.

## CHAPTER XXXVIII.

JESUS CASTS THE SELLERS OUT OF THE TEMPLE.

And the pasch of the Jews was at hand, and Jesus went up to Jerusalem.

And he found in the temple them that sold oxen and sheep and doves, and the changers of money sitting.

And when he had made as it were a scourge of little cords, he drove them all out of the temple, the sheep also and the oxen, and the money of the changers he poured out, and the tables he overthrew.

And to them that sold doves he said: Take these things hence, and make not the house of my Father a house of traffic.—*St. John ii. 13-16.*

*Preparatory Prayer.* Make me realise Thy holy presence, O my God, so that I may be very recollected.

I. I have hitherto, when following Him in spirit, been always much struck by the calm, gentle expression of our Saviour's Countenance. Charity and meekness are His principal characteristics. But to-day He is to be the instrument of His Heavenly Father's justice.

The feast of the Pasch being come, Jesus goes to Jerusalem with His disciples, who have hitherto only been witnesses of His gentleness. They enter the

Temple. I have already followed Jesus ascending, when a little child, the steps of that magnificent edifice. This time He renews, more than ever, the offering of His life to God, His Father; but it is no longer the hidden victim that conceals Himself from the eyes of all. He is about to manifest the truth, to preach penance, and to reprove vice.

At the entrance to the Temple are stationed money changers and vendors of animals destined for sacrifice. Thus to place themselves in the very precincts reserved for ceremonies, was an abuse. Our Lord is about to remind them of the sacrilege of which they are guilty, and the vengeance they deserve for thus profaning the House of God.

II. The Holy Gospel tells us that our Lord, having made a little scourge of cords, drove them all out of the Temple. I can imagine the just and holy anger that animated His Divine Countenance; but, in spite of His indignation, He never loses His self-command. O my Lord and Master, how full of dignity and majesty must Thou not have been, for these men thus to have obeyed Thee, without daring to remonstrate or resist. . . . The money changers' tables are overturned, the sheep and oxen driven out, and the vendors hastily gather together their scattered property.

This is the first act of authority that I see Thee perform, O my God, and Thou dost accomplish it on Thy first arrival at Jerusalem, at the very commencement of Thy public life. Thou didst wish, no doubt, to consecrate by Thy divine example the acts of severity, that all who hold authority from Thee are obliged to perform, whenever the glory of Thy Heavenly Father is concerned.

*Resolution.* I will shew great respect towards all who are in authority over me, and whenever I am reproved or punished by my parents, or those who hold their place, instead of murmuring at their severity, I will submit humbly.

*Prayer.* O my God, vouchsafe to make me understand the duty of submission, grant me the grace to be always docile.

# CHAPTER XXXIX.

## THE ZEAL OF THY HOUSE HATH EATEN ME UP.

And his disciples remembered, that it was written: The zeal of thy house hath eaten me up.—*St. John ii. 17.*

*Preparatory Prayer.* To Thee, O Lord, I consecrate all my thoughts, deign to bless them, and to inspire me with good resolutions.

I. I will now consider the effect, produced upon the disciples by the imposing spectacle of our Lord driving the buyers and sellers from the Temple. Doubtless they were much surprised, for in accompanying Jesus hither, nothing had led them to expect this holy vehemence. On the contrary, their Master's conversation shewed the same solicitude for their welfare, His whole bearing was as calm and meek as usual. They never dreamt for a moment that their gentle Master could be thus animated by holy anger, and were probably terrified when they saw our Lord take the scourge, and drive from the Temple these profaners of His Father's House.

II. Perhaps even some amongst the disciples ventured to blame Jesus' ardour. Others perhaps were shaken in their vocation; the Master appeared to them so different from what He had hitherto been. But suddenly a ray of divine light illuminates the darkness of their understanding; they remember these prophetic words of Holy Scripture: "The zeal of Thy House hath eaten me up," and they are silent.

*Resolution.* What a practical lesson for me, so often prone to follow an unthinking impulse. I will henceforward be careful not to yield to first impressions. I will never judge, unless obliged to do so, and when obliged, never hastily. Whenever I take time to consider, I almost always find that my first impression was wrong.

*Prayer.* Make me understand, O my God, how dangerous it is to judge precipitately, and grant that all my decisions may be conformable to Thine.

## CHAPTER XL.

### NICODEMUS.

And there was a man of the Pharisees, named Nicodemus, a ruler of the Jews.

This man came to Jesus by night, and said to him: Rabbi, we know that thou art come a teacher from God; for no man can do these signs which thou dost, unless God be with him.— *St. John iii. 1, 2.*

*Preparatory Prayer.* O Lord, my God, behold me at Thy Feet, vouchsafe to bless my good intentions.

I. A certain Pharisee named Nicodemus, a man of high rank amongst the Jews, came by night in search of Jesus.

He came by night, because fear of the Jews prevented his openly seeking our Saviour. I can therefore, imagine what precautions he takes to avoid being seen, as he wends his way to the humble dwelling of the Divine Master, Whom he is about to consult. He has no doubt, made secret inquiries as to when he can see Jesus. He quits his home noiselessly, and steals carefully through the streets. Before entering our Lord's house, he makes sure that there is no danger of being discovered.

II. The Divine Master receives him kindly. The Gospel tells us that He explains to this doctor of Israel all the sublime truths that he desires to know, without even addressing him a single word of reproach for his cowardice, in not daring openly to confess his faith.

O Jesus, Thou dost read in the hearts of all; Thou dost receive our good will without reproaching our cowardice. Nicodemus' faith will become stronger and more earnest; and we shall find him, after the death of Jesus, helping Joseph of Arimathea to lay the Saviour in His tomb, braving the fear of the Jews, even when the disciples fly and hide themselves.

*Resolution.* I learn from this that I must not be discouraged, when I feel weak, and tempted to yield to human respect. I must have patience with myself, and overcome my faults little by little, if I have not the courage to make, once for all, a vigorous effort. Above all, I must not yield to discouragement, under pretext that I cannot at once gain the victory.

*Prayer.* My God, I do not struggle alone; deign often to remind me that Thou art by my side, and that Thou hast compassion on my weakness.

## CHAPTER XLI.

### JACOB'S WELL.

He cometh therefore to a city of Samaria, which is called Sichar; near the piece of land which Jacob gave to his son oseph.

Now Jacob's well was there. Jesus therefore being wearied with his journey, sat thus on the well. It was about the sixth hour.—*St. John iv. 5, 6.*

*Preparatory Prayer.* Behold me, O my Saviour, waiting for Thy Voice, teach me Thyself Thy holy law.

I. Jesus, in going from Judea into Galilee, passed through Samaria. The day was excessively hot, and our Saviour, having walked a long distance, was overcome with fatigue. Perhaps Jesus had instructed His disciples on the way; perhaps, according to His custom, He had spent the preceding night in prayer, whilst all around Him slept and took their rest.

His life is hard; in working for His Father's glory He expends His human strength. He does not consider Himself in anything. It is for the glory of His Father and the salvation of souls, that He has come into the world.

The disciples have left Him to go in search of food.

Alone and weary, He pursues His way; but always with the same sweet gravity and calm recollectedness.

II. Jesus, having arrived at Jacob's well, and being wearied with His journey, as the Gospel tells us, sat by the well to rest. O Lord, let me contemplate and adore Thee. Thou appearest to be alone, but angels surround Thee invisibly, heaven looks upon Thee, and even I am present kneeling at Thy Feet. O divine weariness! It is for me, my Saviour, that Thou sufferest thus. Thy brow is covered with sweat, Thy limbs are bruised with fatigue, and all this to save my soul!

O my dear Master, do not permit Thy divine example to be without effect; deign to imprint on my soul the thought of Thy repose at Jacob's well, so that I may learn how to work, and to endure fatigue.

*Resolution.* How often do I not murmur and complain that some duty is too troublesome, that a lesson is interminable, or that some task is too difficult and beyond my strength! I will cast my eyes on Jesus, overcome with fatigue, and will no longer dare to complain.

*Prayer.* Help my weakness, O my God, and grant that I may do with all my heart, and for Thy glory, the duties Thou dost impose upon me.

# CHAPTER XLII.

## THE SAMARITAN WOMAN.

There cometh a woman of Samaria to draw water. Jesus saith to her: Give me to drink.

For his disciples were gone into the city to buy meats.

Then that Samaritan woman saith to him: How dost thou, being a Jew, ask of me to drink, who am a Samaritan woman? For the Jews do not communicate with the Samaritans.

Jesus answered, and said to her: If thou didst know the gift of God, and who is he that saith to thee, Give me to drink; thou perhaps wouldst have asked of him, and he would have given thee living water.

The woman saith to him: Sir, thou has nothing wherein to draw, and the well is deep; from whence then hast thou living water?

Art Thou greater than our father Jacob, who gave us the well, and drank thereof himself, and his children, and his cattle?

Jesus answered, and said to her: Whosoever drinketh of this water shall thirst again; but he that shall drink of the water that I will give him, shall not thirst for ever.

But the water that I will give him, shall become in him a fountain of water springing up into life everlasting.—*St John iv. 7-14.*

. . . . . . . . . .

The woman therefore left her water-pot, and went her way into the city, and saith to the men there:

Come, and see a man who has told me all things whatsoever I have done. Is not he the Christ?

They went therefore out of the city, and came unto him.— *St. John iv. 28-30.*

*Preparatory Prayer.* Dear Lord, deign to make me understand Thy divine words.

I. I have seen Jesus resting by the side of Jacob's well. He knows that He will there have to instruct a soul, and He awaits her coming. A Samaritan woman, clad in bright coloured garments, approaches the well, carrying a pitcher on her head according to the Eastern custom. She advances to draw water, little guessing that she is about to find the source of the water of life and grace. Jesus allows her to approach, and while she bends over the edge of the well to fill her pitcher, addresses to her these simple words, "Give me to drink."

II. At first the woman expresses surprise, but after conversing with her for some time, Jesus makes known Who He is, and what He has come to teach in His Father's name. He also tells her the history of her own life, although this is the first time she has ever seen Him. This revelation of the Divinity of our Lord at once touches the Samaritan and fills her with zeal.

She returns to the city, telling everyone what has happened to her, what Jesus has said, and where He can be seen. Thus she induces many people to go in search of Him to Jacob's well.

In this event of our Saviour's life, which the Gospel relates with many details, I am particularly struck by the words in which Jesus addresses the Samaritan woman, and draws her into conversation: "Give me to drink." Dear Lord, dost Thou not often address these words to me also: "Give me to drink;" for Thou hast taught us to look upon the poor as holding Thy place, and all that we do to them, we do it also to Thee.

When I see poverty to be relieved, it is Thou Thyself Who makest known to me Thy own wants, as when Thou saidst to the Samaritan, "Give me to drink."

*Resolution.* Whenever I have occasion to help the poor, or render some trifling service, I will remember that it is our Lord that asks of me this little alms or act of kindness, and I will respond to His request as far as my parents will allow.

*Prayer.* O Jesus, my dear Master, teach me to profit by Thy divine lessons, make me very faithful in helping Thee in the person of my neighbour, and grant that I may do it with a generous and loving heart.

## CHAPTER XLIII.

### JESUS REMAINS IN SAMARIA.

So when the Samaritans were come to him, they desired him that he would tarry there. And he abode there two days.
And many more believed in him because of his word.
And they said to the woman: We now believe, not for thy saying: for we ourselves have heard him, and know that this is indeed the Saviour of the world.—*St. John iv. 40-42.*

*Preparatory Prayer.* Lord, teach me Thy holy Will; I am listening to Thy Voice, and desire to obey Thy divine teaching.

I. I have read in the Gospel how the Samaritan woman induced many people to follow her, and brought them to Jesus.

No doubt, some only went at first out of curiosity; others perhaps in order to laugh at her credulity and enthusiasm, and to be able to show her how foolish she was, in thus allowing herself to be imposed upon.

They reach Jacob's well; the disciples have rejoined Jesus, and anxiously press Him to eat; but He, instead of taking the food which, no doubt, He greatly needs, forgets His hunger and His weariness, and teaches them that His food is to do the Will of His Father.

II. The Samaritans probably hesitate on seeing

Jesus, and do not venture to interrupt Him, for they are awed by the majestic expression of His Countenance. O Lord, Who canst read in all hearts, Thou didst know well beforehand, what was about to take place at the holy Patriarch's well, and little heeding Thy fatigue, Thou didst forget all, to accomplish Thy divine mission which was to give mankind a heavenly food. These men are touched; they see the first glimmerings of divine light, and longing to know more, they beg of Thee to remain in Samaria, and the Gospel adds, "Jesus abode there two days."

*Resolution.* I should learn from this meditation how much our Lord loves the hearts that seek to be instructed in His divine law. And in yielding to the entreaties of the Samaritans, He wishes to show me that He never refuses to remain with us when we seek Him humbly. I will, therefore, seriously endeavour to know our Lord, and I will often ask of Him this grace.

*Prayer.* O Jesus, teach me how to keep Thee in my heart, as the Samaritans kept Thee in their town.

## CHAPTER XLIV.

### THE RULER OF CAPHARNAUM SEEKS JESUS.

And there was a certain ruler whose son was sick at Capharnaum.

He having heard that Jesus was come from Judea into Galilee, went to him, and prayed him to come down and heal his son: for he was at the point of death.

Jesus therefore said to him: Unless you see signs and wonders you believe not.

The ruler saith to him: Lord, come down before my son die.

Jesus saith to him: Go thy way, thy son liveth. The man believed the word which Jesus said to him, and went his way.— *St. John iv. 46-50.*

*Preparatory Prayer.* My God, do Thou Thyself speak to my heart: I desire to be very docile and recollected.

I. Now there was at Capharnaum a ruler whose son was dangerously ill. His parents, overcome with grief, saw that the case was apparently hopeless, and felt that his end was approaching. His father had heard Jesus spoken of, for the miracle of the water changed to wine had made a great impression in Galilee, and, without knowing the Divine Mission of Jesus Christ, he had been much struck by what he had heard. No doubt, in the midst of his sorrow, he said to himself: If this man is really a prophet, he can as easily heal a sick person as change water into wine, and if he took pity on people, because their wine had run short, it is a proof that he must be very kind-hearted, and will therefore have compassion on my sorrow. I will seek him without delay. How much this poor father must have suffered in quitting his dying son, but he wished to save him, and therefore set out at once.

II. Jesus was on the way to Capharnaum, but must still have been some distance from the town, since it took this man an entire day's journey to meet our Lord. Having encountered Him, the Gospel does not tell us that he cast himself at Jesus' Feet to adore Him.

He had not yet the faith, and was only inspired by an ardent longing for his son's cure. He draws near and entreats Jesus to come and heal his child. Our Lord, Who reads in the depths of hearts, knows that this man does not yet believe, and that he will only have faith, after the cure of his son. "Jesus therefore said to him: *Unless you see signs and wonders you believe not.* The ruler saith to Him: *Lord, come down before that my son die.*" And Jesus, pitying his grief, replies: "Go thy way, thy son liveth." And the Gospel adds that "he believed the word which Jesus said to him and went his way."

What wonderful things are accomplished every day by the omnipotent goodness of God: the regularity of the seasons, for instance, and each succeeding day and night. The grain of corn, too, grows, multiplies and ripens at the proper time. How admirable are all these works of God, and yet how many hearts are closed to the light of faith!

*Resolution.* I will henceforth often think with gratitude of all the wonders that God works even for my temporal good, and to-day I will say my grace after meals with a special devotion.

*Prayer.* Teach me, O Lord, to refer all the wonders of nature and grace to Thy all-powerful goodness.

# CHAPTER XLV.

### THE RULER'S SON IS CURED.

And as he was going down, his servants met him: and they brought word, saying, that his son lived.

He asked therefore of them the hour, wherein he grew better. And they said to him: Yesterday at the seventh hour the fever left him.

The father therefore knew that it was at the same hour, that Jesus said to him: Thy son liveth; and himself believed and his whole house.—*St. John iv. 51-53.*

*Preparatory Prayer.* My God, deign to make me very recollected in Thy divine presence.

I. When Jesus told the ruler of Capharnaum that his son was healed, trusting in our Lord's words, he at once started to return home. How quickly he must have pursued his way, longing to reach the end of his journey. His faith is not yet sufficiently strong to repel certain anxious workings of his reason. Is his son really cured? Jesus may be deceived. How sad will his return be, if his beloved son should be dead! While he is a prey to these sorrowful reflections, he calculates how many hours it is, since he left his child. Thus the unfortunate father proceeds homewards, more and more overcome by his terrible apprehensions.

II. And now he sees in the distance his servants coming to meet him. His uneasiness redoubles, for is it not probable that they are coming to tell him the sad news of his son's death? His heart beats loudly. He is divided between anxiety to join his servants and fear of addressing them, so much does he dread the evil tidings of which he believes them to be the bearers.

At last they come near and tell him that his son lives. Filled with joy, he embraces the faith, and as though to attest more solemnly the miracle that Jesus has wrought, he asks at what hour his son was healed, and the answer proves that the cure took place just at the moment when Jesus said: "Thy son liveth." The Gospel adds "and himself believed and his whole house."

*Resolution.* When I behold the readiness with which this pagan family embrace the faith of Christ, should I not thank our Lord for the great grace of having been born in a Christian country, and in a Christian family. I will to-day perform all my duties in thanksgiving for the gift of faith, and will ask of God to preserve it, and make it increase in my heart.

*Prayer.* Deign, O Lord, to increase my faith.

## CHAPTER XLVI.

### JESUS CURES ST. PETER'S MOTHER-IN-LAW.

And immediately going out of the synagogue, they came into the house of Simon and Andrew, with James and John.

And Simon's wife's mother lay in a fit of a fever: and forthwith they tell him of her.

And coming to her he lifted her up, taking her by the hand: and immediately the fever left her, and she ministered unto them.—*St. Mark i. 29-31.*

*Preparatory Prayer.* Lord Jesus, grant me the pious attention and recollectedness which are necessary in order to meditate properly.

I. One day, whilst He was at Capharnaum, our Lord went to the abode of Simon Peter. How full of joy must not the disciple have been, when Jesus told him that He was going to his house!

He probably sent word quickly that the Master was coming. A great number of persons constantly followed our Lord, eager to hear His words and to witness His miracles, and no doubt amongst the number were many children, attracted by curiosity or by Jesus' loving kindness towards them. Perhaps one of these children was sent with the message, and ran as fast as he could in order to execute his commission as quickly as possible. I can imagine him arriving quite out of breath, and hardly able to speak.

II. What great excitement the news of the Master's coming creates in the house! Jesus must be received with due honour. Every one hastens to make ready for Him, but the preparations are very confused, for Simon's mother-in-law is ill, and as in the East the head of the family is always the person in authority, she it is who habitually orders everything. Now the Gospel tells us that Simon's mother-in-law was in bed with a fever. Simon and Andrew spoke of her to Jesus, and He at once approaching, took her by the hand and made her get up. And at that very moment the fever left her, and she waited upon Him. How astonished and filled with confidence must not all present have been at this sudden cure! I, too, will try and draw the same fruit from this meditation. The Gospel does not tell us that Simon's mother-in-law was in danger of death, but no doubt she was much needed in the little household. Our dear Lord, seeing how useful she would be to her family, deigned to restore her to health. O Jesus, what merciful goodness Thou dost manifest on this occasion! Should I not henceforward confide lovingly to Thee all the needs of my family, even the very smallest.

*Resolution.* I will tell our Lord, with great simplicity and confidence, all that I want for myself and for my parents.

*Prayer.* Thy compassionate Heart is ever open to us, O my God. I will therefore ask Thee for all I need, knowing that, as Thou art my Father, Thou takest interest in all my concerns, and wilt always grant whatever is good for me.

## CHAPTER XLVII.

### JESUS HEALS THE SICK.

And when it was evening after sunset, they brought to him all that were ill and that were possessed with devils :
And all the city was gathered together at the door.
And he healed many that were troubled with divers diseases, and he cast out many devils, and he suffered them not to speak, because they knew him.—*St. Mark i. 32-34.*

*Preparatory Prayer.* My God, be Thou Thyself my Master and my Guide. Oh, teach me to know Thee!

I. The evening of the day on which Jesus cured Saint Peter's mother-in-law, they brought to Him all the sick people of the town.

The news of the miracle, repeated from mouth to mouth, had reached the ears of the sufferers themselves and inspired them with an ardent longing to obtain the same grace. After sunset all the inhabitants assembled before the gates of the town, and waited with anxiety to know the fate of the sick persons who had been brought to Jesus. He laid His Hands upon them and they were all cured. With what compassion the passers-by had looked upon the lame, the sick and the blind, all more or less exhausted by suffering! How eagerly they had helped them to come and lay their sufferings before the compassionate Jesus! Perhaps amongst the number were some who were so discouraged that they did not endeavour to get themselves carried to our Lord, although they longed to be cured. In spite of their remonstrances, their friends had lifted them from off their sick beds and carried them to the Feet of the Divine Physician.

II. I should herein find a very practical lesson for myself. The sickness of the body is an image of the sickness of the soul. There are, unfortunately, in this world a multitude of sinners. I should therefore pray to Jesus to cure them, and often in spite of themselves. For alas! when we have wandered away from God, it often happens that we do not know how to find Him again. Discouragement, indifference and fear combine to keep these sinners, like the sick at Capharnaum, from seeking our Lord. They imagine that nothing can do them any good, or rescue them from their deplorable state.

We must, therefore, bestir ourselves in their behalf, and pray for them, and this even, to a certain extent, in spite of them. If the task be too difficult to admit of the prayer of one person carrying them to Jesus' Feet, then several should unite and pray together.

*Resolution.* I will henceforth remember the souls that I have to bring to Jesus in praying for them, but as my prayers are weak, I will unite myself with all my heart to the Holy Catholic Church.

*Prayer.* My God, I present to Thee all those poor sick souls for whom Thou dost desire that I should specially pray. Heal them, I beg of Thee, in the Name of our Lord Jesus Christ.

## CHAPTER XLVIII.

### JESUS SLEEPS.

And when he entered into the boat, his disciples followed him:
And behold a great tempest arose in the sea, so that the boat was covered with waves, but he was asleep.—*St. Matthew viii. 23, 24.*

*Preparatory Prayer.* Behold me, Lord, at Thy Sacred Feet; deign to instruct me Thyself, and grant that I may be always attentive to Thy words.

I. Our Lord went about teaching through all the cities and little towns. Sometimes He got into a boat and from thence preached to the crowd assembled on the shore of the lake of Galilee. One day that he had been speaking thus to a great number of people, He told the disciples to go over to the other side of the lake, and during the crossing He was overcome with sleep. I see Him lying in the stern of the vessel, exhausted with fatigue, His grave, beautiful Countenance preserving, even in slumber, the sweet expression of union with God His Father, which is habitual to It. The weather being calm, the disciples have no difficulty in managing their boat, which glides rapidly over the water.

II. Grouped together, they converse in low tones, so as not to disturb the Master's rest. No doubt, they speak of the lessons which our Saviour had taught that very day. Some have understood the meaning of His words; others have taken them in a different sense. They argue for a while, and finally agree to ask our Lord, some other time, the explanation of what they have not quite understood, for such was the goodness of Jesus, that His disciples had no hesitation in asking Him questions.

What condescension on the part of God! Should I not blush when I remember how often I am disobliging, *brusque*, or even haughty, when a child younger than myself, a brother, sister or companion, asks me for some little explanation or service, whether for work or play, in which my small experience might be useful? How ashamed I should be to think that I am so unamiable!

*Resolution.* I will not let this feeling of shame be without effect, but will try to be obliging and willing to help, whenever my companions seek my assistance.

*Prayer.* O my God, strengthen me in the resolution I now take of being kind and self-sacrificing in imitation of our Lord Jesus Christ, and deign to remind me of it, whenever an opportunity arises of putting it in practice.

# CHAPTER XLIX.

### JESUS QUELLS THE STORM.

And his disciples came to him, and awaked him, saying: Lord, save us, we perish.

And Jesus saith to them: Why are you fearful, O ye of little faith? Then rising up he commanded the winds, and the sea, and there came a great calm.

But the men wondered, saying: What manner of man is this, for the winds and the sea obey him?—*St. Matt. viii. 25-27.*

*Preparatory Prayer.* My God, speak to my heart, remove far from me all distractions, so that I may listen to Thee attentively.

I. I have seen Jesus sleeping in the boat which bears Him across the lake. At first it is calm, but suddenly the wind rises, and the frail bark is tossed about by the waves, which sometimes even dash over it, filling it with water. The disciples struggle as best they can to manage their boat in the midst of this terrific storm. After a time they become much alarmed, seeing how useless are all their efforts; yet, wherever Jesus is, there is nothing to fear. "Lord," they cry, "save us, we perish."

II. Our Saviour at once awakens, and rising, stands

erect in the storm-tossed bark. He speaks, and the solemn tones of His voice resound above the tumult of the angry winds and waves and the Apostles' cries of terror. He bids the storm to cease, and, says the Holy Gospel, " There came a great calm."

Then turning to His disciples, He says: " Why are you fearful, O ye of little faith ? "

O Lord, Thou mayest well address to us the same question. Deign, then, to increase and make our faith more lively; teach us to ask for it earnestly; and strengthen our devotion to the Holy Church—prefigured by this tempest-tossed bark—in which Thou dost remain, in the midst of us, without ever allowing the storms to prevail against it.

*Resolution.* I will often say to myself, that wherever Jesus is, there is nothing to fear.

*Prayer.* O my God, I know that it is in vain that the Church's enemies rage against her; Jesus, when the time has come, will say to them: " Be silent," and at once there will be a great calm. I beseech Thee, hasten the moment when Thou shalt deliver Thy Church, and glorify the power of Jesus.

## CHAPTER L.

### THE CURE OF THE PARALYTIC.

And they came to him bringing one sick of the palsy, who was carried by four.

And when they could not offer him unto him for the multitude, they uncovered the roof where he was; and opening it they let down the bed wherein the man sick of the palsy lay.

And when Jesus had seen their faith, he saith to the sick of the palsy: Son, thy sins are forgiven thee.—*St. Mark ii. 3-5.*

*Preparatory Prayer.* O my good Master, speak to my heart, I desire to hear and to obey Thee.

I. Jesus was again at Capharnaum, but so many people accompanied Him that the house He was in was quite full. It was much too small, however, for even the space in front of it was insufficient to hold the crowd of persons that were eager to hear His Word. Four men then appeared carrying one sick of the palsy; but they were unable to approach our Lord with their burden. After consulting with his comrades, one of them stays with the sick man, while the others go to speak to the owner of the house. He tells them that there is no help for it, they must get their charge on to the roof (a comparatively easy matter in Eastern houses), and thence, difficult though it be, lower him down. Their faith is great, and they at once set to work.

II. With great trouble these men hoist their sick friend on to the roof, and with still greater trouble they let him down again inside the house, while he, patient and full of hope, does not offer the slightest resistance. Our Lord is there, seated in the midst of an attentive crowd. All of a sudden there is a great stir in the room; the poor paralytic is seen being lowered on his bed from the roof. Jesus, seeing their faith, said to the sick man: "Son, thy sins are forgiven thee;" but knowing the wicked thoughts in the hearts of some of the Pharisees present, He at once added: "Which is easier to say: Thy sins are forgiven thee; or to say: Arise and walk?" And then turning to the sick man: "I say to thee, arise, take up thy bed and go into thy house." And immediately he arose and went his way, and all present were filled with admiration.

*Resolution.* I will never forget these words of the Gospel: "Jesus seeing their faith." It was the faith of these men that obtained the paralytic's cure. Oh, what a lesson for me! I must have faith and confidence in order to obtain the graces I ask.

*Prayer.* My God, I believe; increase, I beseech Thee, my faith.

# CHAPTER LI.

## THE CALL OF SAINT MATTHEW.

And when Jesus passed on from thence, he saw a man sitting in the custom-house, named Matthew: and he saith to him: Follow me. And he arose up, and followed him.—*St. Matthew ix. 9.*

*Preparatory Prayer.* O my God, help me to hear Thy Voice, and to obey Thy call with submission.

I. Jesus, having departed from thence, as the Gospel tells us, after the cure of the paralytic, saw a man called Matthew, sitting at the custom-house, and said to him: "Follow Me:" and Matthew arose and followed Him.

This man was one of the twelve Apostles, and also an Evangelist. This simple description of his call by Jesus is taken from his own Gospel. His usual employment was to help in making up the revenue returns and accounts, an occupation of by no means a refining nature. He was, in fact, a publican, one of a class usually devoid of honesty, and therefore justly despised. But the moment he heard the Voice of Jesus, he left everything and obeyed at once. We can imagine how great must have been the astonishment of his relations and those associated with him in his work, when he declared that he was about to abandon his old employment, and seek no other but that of following and obeying Jesus.

II. The Gospel tells us that the moment St. Matthew heard our Lord's call, he at once, without waiting to reflect, arose and followed his new Master. So in the same way, no doubt, did he act in going frankly and without any human respect, to tell his old employers of his sudden resolve. Many there must have been who blamed him: but Jesus had spoken, and nothing could shake his determination. What a grand example of fidelity to the Voice of God! Such a striking instance of a divine call is not often met with: yet Jesus speaks to the conscience of each one of us, and that at every instant. Do I not often hear our dear Lord tell me to follow Him? Are not good inclinations, or the desire to sacrifice our self-love or our own will, or to mortify ourselves according to the measure of our strength and age, one and all calls from God?

To obey Him is to follow Him.

*Resolution.* The time will surely come for me, when I shall have much to suffer, when good will become irksome, and evil easy. I must therefore prepare myself betimes by small daily struggles. I will to-day do promptly and joyfully, whatever Almighty God shall ask of me, whether through my parents, my superiors, or my own conscience.

*Prayer.* O Jesus, help me to imitate the promptitude of St. Matthew. He arose and followed Thee. Never allow me to reason, or to repel Thy inspiration, but make me always remember Thy words, "Follow Me." May I always follow Thee.

## CHAPTER LII.

### THE HEM OF JESUS' GARMENT.

And there cometh one of the rulers of the synagogue named Jairus: and seeing him (Jesus), falleth down at his feet,

And he besought him much, saying: My daughter is at the point of death, come, lay thy hand upon her, that she may be safe, and may live.

And he went with him, and a great multitude followed him, and they thronged him.

And a woman who was under an issue of blood twelve years,

And had suffered many things from many physicians, and had spent all that she had, and was nothing the better, but rather worse:

When she heard of Jesus, came in the crowd behind him, and touched his garment:

For she said: If I shall touch but his garment, I shall be whole.

And forthwith the fountain of her blood was dried up: and she felt in her body that she was healed of the evil.

And immediately Jesus, knowing in himself the virtue that had proceeded from him, turning to the multitude, said: Who hath touched my garments?

And his disciples said to him: Thou seest the multitude thronging thee, and sayest thou: Who hath touched me !

And he looked about to see her who had done this.

But the woman fearing and trembling, knowing what was

done in her, came and fell before him, and told him all the truth.

And he said to her: Daughter, thy faith hath made thee whole: go in peace, and be thou whole of thy disease.—*St. Mark v. 22-34.*

*Preparatory Prayer.* O my God, deign to make me understand what Thou teachest.

I. Jairus, one of the rulers of the Synagogue (the Jewish churches were so called, synagogue being the Greek for an assembly) came to Jesus, and threw himself at His Feet, saying: "My daughter is dying, come and lay Thy hands upon her and she will live." Jesus therefore went with him, closely followed by a large crowd. Amongst those present was a poor woman who, though also earnestly longing to be cured, was yet afraid to attempt to stop our Lord on His way to the ruler's house. A struggle was going on within her between her timidity and her desire to be healed.

II. Her faith then suggests to her the thought that if she could but touch His garment she would be cured. She enters the thick of the crowd, and tries to get near to Jesus, which she succeeds in doing, and, without a word and unnoticed, she touches our Lord's garment. "And immediately Jesus," so says the Gospel, "knowing in Himself the virtue that had proceeded from Him, turning to the multitude, said: 'Who hath touched My garments?'" Thus the poor woman, who did not even dare to ask her cure from Jesus, found herself most unexpectedly discovered. She did not hesitate, however, but throwing herself at the Feet of her Lord, confessed the truth. Jesus said to her: "Daughter, thy faith hath made thee whole, go thy way in peace," and on the instant she was cured.

How great must have been her joy! She arises full of life, cured and comforted. Her heart is the more touched by the goodness of Jesus, inasmuch as she feared to have been severely reproved.

*Resolution.* Let me draw a lesson from the contemplation of this poor woman's great happiness. Jesus, in working this miracle by the mere contact of His clothes, shows me the power with which He endows relics. In praising this woman for the faith which made her say, "If I can but touch His garment I shall be cured," He also praises those who were later to possess the same faith. I will therefore have the greatest respect for the relics of our Lord, the true Cross, the Crown of Thorns and the Nails, and also for the relics of the Saints.

*Prayer.* O my God, grant me a confidence, full of respect and faith, in the holy relics which the Church proposes to our veneration.

# CHAPTER LIII.

## THE RAISING OF THE DAUGHTER OF JAIRUS TO LIFE.

While he was yet speaking, some come from the ruler of the synagogue's house, saying: Thy daughter is dead: why dost thou trouble the Master any farther?

But Jesus having heard the word that was spoken, saith to the ruler of the synagogue: Fear not, only believe.

And he admitted not any man to follow him, but Peter, and James, and John the brother of James.

And they come to the house of the ruler of the synagogue, and he seeth a tumult, and people weeping and wailing much.

And going in, he saith to them: Why make you this ado, and weep? the damsel is not dead but sleepeth.

And they laughed him to scorn. But he having put them all out, taketh the father and the mother of the damsel, and them that were with him, and entereth in where the damsel was lying.

And taking the damsel by the hand, he saith to her: Talitha cumi, which is, being interpreted, Damsel (I say to thee) arise;

And immediately the damsel rose up, and walked: and she was twelve years old: and they were astonished with a great astonishment.

And he charged them strictly that no man should know it: and commanded that something should be given her to eat.— *St. Mark v. 35 to 43.*

*Preparatory Prayer.* My God, enable me, I beseech Thee, to understand what Thou teachest me.

I. The cure of the poor woman, who touched our Lord's garment, delayed His progress a few moments, and before He had finished speaking, some servants came with haste from Jairus' house, and said to him: "Thy daughter is dead, why dost thou trouble the Master any farther?" But Jesus, full of compassion, and grieved, no doubt, at the sudden way in which the unfortunate father heard the terrible news, said to him at once: "Fear not: only believe," that is to say, have sufficient faith to believe that I can as easily raise the dead to life as cure the sick. Nevertheless Jesus wishes to try his faith: and so, without giving any explanation, He simply says: "Only believe." Jairus, humble and confident, conducts our Lord to his house. Many people are already, according to the Jewish custom, weeping and lamenting around the dead. The poor mother is there, clasping in her arms the lifeless body of her child. To the very last she had hoped that Jesus would come in time to cure her daughter. But now all is over.

II. Our Lord approaches, and enjoins silence. He enters the chamber of death, and going up to the bed where the lifeless body of the girl (who was twelve years old) is lying, the kind Master takes her by the hand and says: "Maid, arise." And she at once arose and began to walk: and He commanded that she should be given to eat. This He did, no doubt, to show her parents, who were lost in astonishment, that their daughter was really living.

What a wonderful scene. Observe the calm Majesty of the Redeemer, the joy of the parents, the simplicity of the child, who comes back to life but half-conscious of the miracle wrought upon her! Is not this return to life a figure of what takes place in my soul, when God restores me to the life of grace by sacramental absolution?

*Resolution.* I will always endeavour to leave the Confessional in the same dispositions as this young girl and the witnesses of her return to life, that is to say, adoring and blessing Jesus for the miracle He has worked in restoring me to the life of grace.

*Prayer.* O my God, make me fully understand, I beg of Thee, the greatness of this rising again which I am unfortunately only too disposed to make light of and consider without gratitude.

# CHAPTER LIV.

## ST. MARY MAGDALEN IN SIMON'S HOUSE.

And behold a woman that was in the city a sinner, when she knew that he sat at meat in the Pharisee's house, brought an alabaster box of ointment:

And standing behind at his feet, she began to wash his feet with tears, and wiped them with the hairs of her head, and kissed his feet, and anointed them with the ointment.

And the Pharisee, who had invited him, seeing it, spoke within himself, saying: This man if he were a prophet, would know surely who and what manner of woman this is that toucheth him: that she is a sinner.

And Jesus answering, said to him: Simon, I have somewhat to say to thee. But he said: Master, say it.

A certain creditor had two debtors: the one owed five hundred pence, and the other fifty.

And whereas they had not wherewith to pay, he forgave them both. Which therefore of the two loveth him most?

Simon answering said: I suppose that he, to whom he forgave most. And he said to him: Thou hast judged rightly.

And turning to the woman, he said unto Simon: Dost thou see this woman? I entered into thy house, thou gavest me no water for my feet; but she with tears hath washed my feet, and with her hairs hath wiped them. . . .

Wherefore I say to thee: Many sins are forgiven her, because she hath loved much. But to whom less is forgiven, he loveth less.

And he said to her: Thy sins are forgiven thee.—*St. Luke vii. 37-44 and 47, 48.*

*Preparatory Prayer.* O Lord, I beg of Thee, to speak to me Thyself, for I earnestly desire to listen to Thee attentively.

I. Simon, the Pharisee, having besought Jesus to come to his house, our Lord went to sup with him. Almost at the same moment, a woman, who had, so far, only given bad example, also entered the house. This was Mary Magdalen, who, young and handsome, was a prey to vanity and the evil passions that follow closely in its wake. A few words of Jesus, previously heard by her, were, however, sufficient to touch her heart, and following the impulse of grace, she had already begun to consider the state of her conscience, and to abhor her past sins; but a great struggle took place, before she had the courage to go to Jesus and reform her life. She however conquered, and in future never refused anything to our Lord. A pious author, the Père Nouet, in his book of Meditations, speaking of her, says: "What wonder is it that she should lay aside her handsome dresses, her jewels and her gold? Do not we throw everything out of the window, when the house is on fire? Jesus had set her heart ablaze with the fire of divine love; she could not therefore fail to give up all her worldly ornaments."

II. Magdalen, amongst the other luxuries, which in her past life of ease and pleasure she had indulged in to the full, had some of the choicest Eastern perfumes. The best of these she now destines for our Lord, and in His honour takes a beautiful alabaster vessel, filled with rare spices, to Simon's house. There, humbly prostrate before our Saviour, while her sobs betray her emotion, and her tears of repentance fall upon the Feet of Jesus, she pours her perfumes over Them in silence, wiping Them with her long luxuriant hair.

After a time, Jesus reading the wicked thoughts of the Pharisees, breaks the silence and says to the master of the house: "Simon, I have something to say to thee." He then makes him understand by a beautiful parable, that the generous love of this woman, which induces her to sacrifice everything for God, should make us forget her past life, in this her act of love, and He adds: "Many sins are forgiven her, because she has loved much."

*Resolution.* Knowing how our Lord rewards those who love Him, I will try to enkindle in my heart the fire of charity, by making daily acts of divine love, and asking Jesus to make me love Him more.

*Prayer.* O my God, forgive me all my sins, so that I may love Thee more: and make me love Thee more, so that Thou mayst forgive me all my sins.

# CHAPTER LV.

### JESUS CHOOSETH THE TWELVE APOSTLES.

And it came to pass in those days, that he went out into a mountain to pray, and he passed the whole night in the prayer of God.

And when day was come, he called unto him his disciples: and he chose twelve of them (whom also he named Apostles). —*St. Luke vi. 12, 13.*

*Preparatory Prayer.* O Lord, deign to teach me Thyself, and help me to understand Thy teaching.

I. I have already seen how Jesus had called many disciples in different circumstances, and amongst others, I have noticed St. Matthew's ready response to His summons, "Follow Me."

A small chosen band, then, followed our Lord in His wanderings through Galilee, and profited by His divine teaching. To-day I will meditate on what happened when Jesus chose the twelve Apostles.

First of all, the word Apostle, which means a messenger, explains their mission; but before choosing them, see how our Lord prays. "And it came to pass in those days, that He went out into a mountain to pray, and He passed the whole night in the prayer of God. And when day was come, He called unto Him

His disciples: and He chose twelve of them (whom also He named Apostles)."

Let us learn from this, the practical lesson of always praying before taking any decision, or commencing any work.

II. Let us not say, with a levity suitable to our idleness, that such a plan is all very well in the case of important decisions, or that, though it may be a help to us later, it is not necessary for us at present. That is a great mistake. Youth has its duties as well as age. For example, it is our duty to learn our lessons, however troublesome they may be at times, and cheerfully to obey the commands of those in authority over us.

Such being the case, where shall we get the necessary help, if not from Jesus, Who, by praying as He did on the mountain, teaches us that He will hear our prayers, if only we raise our hearts to Him, before the principal actions of our childhood ?

It will help us to understand the necessity of prayer, if we consider how, after a long day's journey, our Lord retired to pray, while His disciples sought the necessary rest. Alone He ascends a rocky path, and in a secluded spot prostrates Himself in the presence of God.

O Jesus, what an admirable prayer must Thine have been !

We it was, who should have prayed, because the Apostles, Thou wast about to choose, were to teach us the truth. Thou wert then thinking of all and each of us. But why should we speak of the past? Dost Thou not still pray unceasingly for us all? Art Thou not ever in the tabernacle, and is not the Holy Eucharist one continual prayer for all mankind?

*Resolution.* I will to-day offer my principal actions to Almighty God, by constantly raising up my heart to Him.

*Prayer.* O my God, teach me to unite my intention to that of Jesus Christ, so that His perpetual intercession in the tabernacle may make amends for my poor prayers.

## CHAPTER LVI.

### THE MISSION OF THE APOSTLES.

Then he saith to his disciples : The harvest indeed is great, but the labourers are few.

Pray ye therefore the Lord of the harvest, that he send forth labourers into his harvest.—*St. Matthew ix. 37, 38.*

. . . . . . . . . . . .

And having called his twelve disciples together, he gave them power over unclean spirits, to cast them out and to heal all manner of diseases, and all manner of infirmities,

And the names of the twelve apostles are these : The first : Simon who is called Peter, and Andrew his brother,

James the son of Zebedee, and John his brother, Philip and Bartholomew, Thomas and Matthew the publican, and James the son of Alpheus, and Thaddeus,

Simon the Cananean, and Judas Iscariot, who also betrayed him.—*St. Matthew x. 1-4.*

*Preparatory Prayer.* O my God, help me to be recollected, in order to derive more fruit from Thy teaching.

I. Our Lord, after the prayer to His Father, returns to His disciples, and in the words of the Evangelist, says to them : "The harvest indeed is great, but the labourers are few. Pray ye therefore the Lord of the harvest, that He send forth labourers into His harvest."

He then gave them power to cast out devils, and heal all sorts of infirmities and diseases. The chosen twelve were Simon Peter and his brother Andrew, who left their boat, as we have seen, James the son of Zebedee, and his brother John, who left their father to follow Jesus, Philip, Bartholomew, Thomas, Matthew the publican, who at once gave up his employment when Jesus called him, James the son of Alpheus, and Thaddeus, Simon the Cananean and Judas Iscariot, who betrayed our Lord.

Then Jesus gave His commands to His new envoys. He told them how they were to preach the joyful news in His Name, and fortified them against indifference, disdain, contradictions and sufferings.

II. Alas! among the chosen twelve there was one who has since become an object of such deep execration, that now no greater insult can be conceived than to call any one Judas. I will therefore, at present, only consider the remaining eleven, whose names have come down, from generation to generation, glorified with the titles of Saints and Martyrs. I will renew my respect for, and my faith and confidence in the intercession of these holy and valiant Soldiers of Christ. I will call to mind what I already know, and will strive to learn more of their glorious lives and martyrdom. How beautiful and full of interest are the lives of the Saints! I will meditate, too, on the words of our Lord to the Apostles:

"And you shall be brought before governors, and

before kings for My sake, for a testimony to them and to the gentiles.

But when they shall deliver you up, take no thought how or what to speak : for it shall be given you in that hour what to speak. . . .

. . . And fear ye not them that kill the body, and are not able to kill the soul : but rather fear him that can destroy both soul and body into hell."

*Resolution.* I will often examine myself on the subject of fear, and ask Almighty God to make me dread sin alone.

*Prayer.* O my God, deign, in Thy supreme power, to make me fear nothing but Thy justice. Enable me to follow the example of Thy Saints, and not to yield to human respect, either now in small things, or later in the more serious matters of life.

## CHAPTER LVII.

### THE CENTURION'S SERVANT.

And when he had entered into Capharnaum, there came to him a centurion, beseeching him,

And saying: Lord, my servant lieth at home sick of the palsy, and is grievously tormented.

And Jesus saith to him: I will come and heal him.

And the centurion making answer, said: Lord, I am not worthy that thou shouldst enter under my roof: but only say the word, and my servant shall be healed.

For I also am a man subject to authority, having under me soldiers; and I say to this: Go, and he goeth: and to another, Come, and he cometh: and to my servant, Do this, and he doth it.

And Jesus hearing this, marvelled; and said to them that followed him: Amen, I say to you, I have not found so great faith in Israel.

And I say to you that many shall come from the east and the west, and shall sit down with Abraham, and Isaac, and Jacob in the kingdom of heaven:

But the children of the kingdom shall be cast out into the exterior darkness: there shall be weeping and gnashing of teeth.

And Jesus said to the centurion: Go, and as thou hast believed, so be it done to thee. And the servant was healed at the same hour.—*St. Matthew viii. 5 to 13.*

*Preparatory Prayer.* My Saviour Jesus, I am

listening, speak to me, teach me, and deign to touch my heart.

I. "And when Jesus had entered into Capharnaum, there came to Him a centurion, beseeching Him,

And saying: Lord, my servant lieth at home sick of the palsy, and is grievously tormented.

And Jesus saith to him: I will come and heal him.

And the centurion making answer, said: Lord, I am not worthy that thou shouldst enter under my roof: but only say the word, and my servant shall be healed.

For I also am a man subject to authority, having under me soldiers, and I say to this: Go, and he goeth: and to another, Come, and he cometh: and to my servant, Do this, and he doth it." But Thou O Lord, Who art Omnipotent, canst, with much greater right, command the disease to leave my servant.

Here is a great example of faith and humility: the centurion, believing in Jesus' power to do what he wishes, humbles himself before Him, and declares himself unworthy to receive his God in his house.

II. Therefore it was, as the Holy Gospel tells us, that our Lord praised him to His disciples, and then turning to him, as he was respectfully waiting for His answer, said, in a tone of kindness that incomparably enhanced the gift: "Go, and as thou hast believed, so be it done to thee." And the servant was healed at the same hour. One almost fancies one can see the good centurion hasten joyfully away to his house, and hear him relate to his servant, whom he finds quite cured, all the details of his interview with our Lord. Not only did Jesus commend his faith and humility, but the Church has set him up as an example to us all, by making us repeat, at the moment of Holy Communion, the words: "Lord, I am not worthy Thou shouldst enter under my roof; say only the word and my soul shall be healed."

*Resolution.* I will try always to repeat these holy words with great faith, and endeavour to appreciate their meaning.

*Prayer.* O my God, give me the faith and the humility of the centurion, whenever I have the happiness to receive Thy Divine Body.

## CHAPTER LVIII.

### THE WIDOW'S SON.

And it came to pass afterwards, that he went into a city that is called Naim; and there went with him his disciples, and a great multitude.

And when he came nigh to the gate of the city, behold a dead man was carried out, the only son of his mother; and she was a widow: and a great multitude of the city was with her.

Whom when the Lord had seen, being moved with mercy towards her he said to her: Weep not.

And he came near, and touched the bier. (And they that carried it stood still.) And he said: Young man, I say to thee, arise.

And he that was dead sat up, and began to speak. And he gave him to his mother.

And there came a fear on them all: and they glorified God saying: A great prophet is risen up among us: and, God hath visited his people.—*St. Luke vii. 11-16.*

*Preparatory Prayer.* O my God, behold me at Thy Feet, deign to instruct me.

I. Our Lord is going to Naim, and is accompanied by a great crowd of people: presently He is met by a funeral coming out of the city, and a way is made to allow it to pass. Jesus was, no doubt, the first to set the example of respectful silence, while His looks betokened sympathy and showed how He was praying. The funeral procession filed along before Him. First came the mourners and musicians, according to the custom of the Jews, then the friends and relations of the deceased, and finally the coffin which, following the Eastern practice, was a sort of stretcher, on which the body was carried fully dressed. The corpse was that of a young man, whose peaceful and innocent expression was more suggestive of sleep than of death. But alas, the anguish of the poor mother, arrayed in her long robe of mourning, left no room for doubt, as she walked by her son's side without seeming to see or hear anything! When our Lord saw the poor disconsolate mother, He was touched with compassion, and said to her: "*Weep not.* And He came near, and touched the bier. And they that carried it stood still. And He said: *Young man, I say to thee, arise.* And he that was dead sat up, and began to speak. And He gave him to his mother."

Who could describe the joy and gratitude of the poor mother? She threw herself at Jesus' Feet to thank Him, while all present, as the Gospel tells us, glorified God.

II. I, too, will meditate on these words, and will try, in my humble way, to glorify God by praising His Infinite goodness. O Jesus, grant me some share of Thy sympathy for those in suffering, so that I may learn to love Thee more. In Thy other miracles, the afflicted came to Thee to ask for mercy, but on this occasion Thou Thyself didst take the initiative by saying, "Weep not."

*Resolution.* I will often try to excite in myself feelings of gratitude towards God, and thank Him for His gifts and graces.

*Prayer.* O Jesus, Who, on account of the anguish of this poor mother, didst restore her son, increase my confidence in Thy tender mercy and compassion.

## CHAPTER LIX.

### JOHN'S TWO DISCIPLES.

And John called to him two of his disciples, and sent them to Jesus, saying: Art thou he that art to come, or look we for another?

And when the men were come unto him, they said: John the Baptist hath sent us to thee, saying: Art thou he that art to come, or look we for another?

(And in that same hour, he cured many of their diseases, and hurts, and evil spirits, and to many that were blind he gave sight.)

And answering, he said to them: Go and relate to John what you have heard and seen: The blind see, the lame walk, the lepers are made clean, the deaf hear, the dead rise again, to the poor the gospel is preached:

And blessed is he whosoever shall not be scandalized in me. —*St. Luke vii. 19-23.*

*Preparatory Prayer.* O my God, make me obedient and attentive, and do Thou Thyself teach me what to do.

I. St. John the Baptist, even when in prison, being allowed by Herod to see his disciples, lost no opportunity of instructing, and so winning souls to God. He noticed, however, that his disciples, out of a blind affection for himself, were unwilling to believe in the superiority of our Lord, or to regard Him as the Messiah.

Still, however, the fame of Jesus' miracles spread over all Galilee, so that John took advantage of it to convince his disciples. He sent two of them to ask our Lord, "Art thou He that art to come?" This he did not do for himself, as he knew perfectly that Jesus was the Son of God, for on the banks of the Jordan, when the Son of Mary humbly came to him to be baptised, St. John at once said: "Behold, The Lamb of God." He however wished our Lord to declare Himself to the two messengers.

II. These two messengers, then, sensible of the honour of being sent to one whose fame was great, set out with speed, for curiosity, as well as obedience, made them anxious to see Jesus. Moreover they probably expected to ascertain the truth, or expose the imposture, if St. John should be mistaken. When they reached the place where Jesus was, they discovered where to find Him, but, doubtless, they did not expect to meet Him in the midst of a crowd of poor, infirm and sick people. Jesus is, however, so surrounded by these unfortunates that He can hardly get from one to the other. St. John's disciples deliver their message: but our Lord simply continues His work of healing the sick, before replying: "Go and relate to John what you have heard and seen: The blind see, the lame walk, the lepers are made clean, the deaf hear, the dead rise again, to the poor the Gospel is preached."

Such a proof of the Divinity of Jesus was overwhelming. With joyful faith and admiration St. John's disciples hastily returned to him with the good news of what they had seen.

*Resolution.* Our Lord answers the question, "Who art Thou?" by His works. I, also, will ever try to show by my actions that I am a Christian.

*Prayer.* O God, grant that all the actions of my life may be worthy of my proud title of Christian.

## CHAPTER LX.

### THE SOWER.

And when a very great multitude was gathered together and hastened out of the cities unto him, he spoke by a similitude:
The sower went out to sow his seed: and as he sowed some fell by the wayside, and it was trodden down, and the fowls of the air devoured it.—*St. Luke viii. 4, 5.*

*Preparatory Prayer.* O Lord, be Thou near me, and enlighten my understanding.

I. Our Lord, being one day, in the course of His journeyings through the cities and towns, surrounded by an immense crowd, proposed to them the following parable:—

"The sower went out to sow his seed: and as he sowed some fell by the wayside, and it was trodden down, and the fowls of the air devoured it."

And Jesus, in His patience and goodness, Himself thus explained His meaning: "The seed is the Word of God.

"And they by the wayside are they that hear: then the devil cometh, and taketh the word out of their heart, lest believing they should be saved."

The farmer, it is true, cannot sow his seed until the land has been made ready for it, and this can only be done by much toil and labour, often rendered doubly burdensome by the intense heat of the sun.

II. Well, all this labour is only an image of the pains and trouble, that Jesus takes, in His paternal solicitude for me, to prepare my soul to receive His divine Word. The care that has been bestowed on me in my infancy, and the good example I have had, have all formed part, though I may never have been conscious of it, of our Lord's divine work in me. Therefore if I get into the habit of forgetting these great favours, or at least of not noticing, or ever thinking of them, do I not also become the prey of the devil, who, as in the parable, follows the sower and steals the seed away? And why does he come, if not lest the seed should bear fruit in my heart?

*Resolution.* I will always be as attentive to, and try to remember, as though it were the Word of God, the religious advice and instruction I receive, and will frequently thank Almighty God for it.

*Prayer.* O my God, I thank Thee for all the gifts Thou hast bestowed upon me in my childhood. Make me understand that fidelity to grace is the only way to obtain fresh favours.

## CHAPTER LXI.

### THE ROCKY SOIL.

And other some fell upon a rock: and as soon as it was sprung up it withered away, because it had no moisture.—*St. Luke viii. 6.*

*Preparatory Prayer.* My Good Master, teach me Thyself, I will listen to Thee attentively.

I. I will again consider how Jesus goes on to explain the parable of the sower to the multitude, and, like them, listen to Him with great attention.

"And other some fell upon a rock: and as soon as it was sprung up it withered away, because it had no moisture. . . . Now, they upon the rock, are they who when they hear, receive the word with joy: and these have no roots; who believe for a while, and in time of temptation fall away."

This picture, drawn by our Lord, reminds us of the tufts of grass, or even flowers, which grow on the all but barren spots by the road-side, where stray seeds may have chanced to fall, but which, though of speedy growth, live but a few days, and then wither away owing to the heat of the sun.

II. Our Lord, by this parable, wishes to make us understand that we must not only receive His Word with joy, but that we must cherish it, and, by persevering, make it bear fruit. Yesterday, in considering the work of the husbandman, I meditated on what Jesus had done for me in my childhood. To-day the same parable, listened to with joy, should call to mind my First Communion. How fervent was I then, and how faithful to my religious duties! But surely our Lord did not wish me to stop there? No, I must still be mindful of the seed I then received; I must continue to be faithful, and protect the young shoots from withering away and perishing. And how shall I do this?

*Resolution.* I will frequently in my prayers, and especially at Mass and Holy Communion, ask for the grace of perseverance.

*Prayer.* O God, I have unfortunately been only too remiss in asking Thee for an increase of Thy divine love. Grant me now that I may persevere in it, so that it may one day lead me to Thee in Heaven.

## CHAPTER LXII.

### THE THORNS AND THE GOOD GROUND.

And other some fell among thorns, and the thorns growing up with it, choked it.

And other some fell upon good ground: and being sprung up, yielded fruit a hundred-fold.—*St. Luke viii. 7, 8.*

*Preparatory Prayer.* Once more at Thy Feet, O Lord, do I wish to study the parable of the sower.

I. "And other some fell among thorns, and the thorns growing up with it, choked it. . . . And that which fell among thorns, are they who have heard, and going their way, are choked with the cares and riches and pleasures of this life, and yield no fruit." The barren soil, I know, produces nothing but brambles and thorns, which exhaust it and render it useless. There are, unfortunately, too many useless persons in the world, who have not learnt to profit by our Lord's teachings. But the Good Master adds: "And other some fell upon good ground: and being sprung up yielded fruit a hundred-fold. . . .

"But that on the good ground, are they, who, in a good and perfect heart, hearing the word, keep it, and bring forth fruit in patience."

The beautiful golden cornfields before the harvest,

with their rich and waving ears of wheat, show what a quantity of sheaves good soil can produce, and how it yields a hundred-fold and more, for in time the corn becomes flour and the food both of the rich and poor.

II. Nothing could better illustrate how our hearts may, and should, bear fruit after receiving the Word of God. But although our good actions will never attain the perfection, or the number that our Lord expects, still we must not lose courage, but remember that, if we work willingly, Jesus will Himself help us to reach the standard He requires of us. Our efforts must of necessity be proportionate to our strength, but if we labour now, we shall find that, as we grow older, we shall produce more fruit.

*Resolution.* Whenever I feel myself inclined, through pleasure or distraction, to forget my duty or stifle a good resolution, I will struggle with all my strength against the temptation.

*Prayer.* My God, deign to make the seed, Thou hast sown in my heart, bear the fruit. Thou didst expect of it.

## CHAPTER LXIII.

### JESUS AND THE HOLY WOMEN.

And it came to pass afterwards, that he travelled through the cities and towns, preaching and evangelizing the kingdom of God : and the twelve with him,
And certain women who had been healed of evil spirits and infirmities ; Mary who is called Magdalen, out of whom seven devils were gone forth,
And Joanna the wife of Chusa, Herod's steward, and Susanna, and many others who ministered unto him of their substance.—*St. Luke viii. 1-3.*

*Preparatory Prayer.* O my God, grant me a truer knowledge of Thy Divine Son Jesus, so that I may follow Him more closely, and love Him more ardently.

I. Jesus was travelling "through the cities and towns, preaching and evangelizing the kingdom of God : and the twelve with Him, And certain women who had been healed of evil spirits and infirmities, Mary who is called Magdalen, out of whom seven devils were gone forth, And Joanna the wife of Chusa, Herod's steward, and Susanna, and many others who ministered unto him of their substance." Here, then, do I again find Magdalen whom I have seen at Jesus' Feet in Simon's house. Learned writers tell us that the seven devils, mentioned in the Scripture, are the evil passions that our Lord expelled at her conversion. These women whom Jesus had healed, no doubt followed Him out of gratitude. Ought not I too, to be imbued with a deep feeling of gratitude towards God? What graces have I not received? In baptism the devil was driven away from me, and was still further removed by holy absolution, and especially by the presence of Jesus, when at my First Communion, and so frequently since, He has deigned to come into my heart. What have I done in return? What ought I not to do to show that I am not ungrateful?

II. I will profit by the example of these holy women. They ministered to our Lord and His Apostles, and by so doing contributed to the divine work. A pious author, indeed, tells us that "they deserve their share of the recompense, for, inasmuch as the Apostle could not preach, if he had to busy himself about the necessaries of life, they who supply his wants, may be said to preach by his mouth." *

I, too, can enjoy the same privilege, for, though only chosen souls are allowed to follow our missionaries in China or elsewhere, yet, thanks to the works of the Propagation of the Faith, and of the Holy Childhood, all Christians can share in the reward of these zealous apostles. Have I ever yet properly considered the great resemblance between Jesus preaching in Galilee

* Le Père de Ligny, *Histoire de la Vie de Notre-Seigneur Jésus-Christ.*

and the missionaries in those countries where His Name is unknown?

*Resolution.* O my God, I promise in future to be regular in my small weekly contribution to the Propagation of the Faith, so as, imitating the example of the holy women, to help on Thy work, and merit a share in the Apostles' reward.

*Prayer.* O Jesus, Who didst tell us to pray that the Lord of the harvest might send forth labourers, increase the number and the fervour of our missionaries, and inspire all Christians to assist their work by prayer and almsgiving.

## CHAPTER LXIV.

### THE WHEAT AND THE COCKLE.

Another parable he proposed to them, saying: The kingdom of heaven is likened to a man that sowed good seed in his field;

But while men were asleep, his enemy came and oversowed cockle among the wheat, and went his way.

And when the blade was sprung up, and had brought forth fruit, then appeared also the cockle. And the servants of the good man of the house coming said to him: Sir, didst thou not sow good seed in thy field? Whence then hath it cockle?

And he said to them: An enemy hath done this. And the servants said to him: Wilt thou that we go and gather it up? And he said: No: lest perhaps gathering up the cockle, you root up the wheat also together with it.

Suffer both to grow until the harvest, and in the time of the harvest I will say to the reapers: Gather up first the cockle, and bind it into bundles to burn, but the wheat gather ye into my barn.—*St. Matthew xiii. 24-30.*

*Preparatory Prayer.* Make known to me, O Lord, Thy goodness, in order that I may understand and love Thee.

I. As our Lord said in this parable, "The kingdom of heaven is likened to a man that sowed good seed in his field. But while men were asleep, his enemy came and oversowed cockle among the wheat, and went his way." But the master did not allow his servants to gather up the cockle then, but said to them: "Suffer both to grow until the harvest, and in the time of the harvest I will say to the reapers: Gather up first the cockle, and bind it into bundles to burn, but the wheat gather ye into my barn." And Jesus further explains the parable. "He that soweth the good seed is the Son of man. And the field is the world. And the good seed are the children of the kingdom. And the cockle are the children of the wicked one. And the enemy that sowed them is the devil. But the harvest is the end of the world. And the reapers are the angels. Even as cockle therefore is gathered up, and burnt with fire: so shall it be at the end of the world. The Son of man shall send His angels, and they shall gather out of His kingdom all scandals, and them that work iniquity: And shall cast them into the furnace of fire: there shall be weeping and gnashing of teeth."

II. Almighty God shows me in this parable, which He has so clearly explained, how the good and the wicked are mixed up in the world, and how the latter are punished, while the former are rewarded, hereafter. Is not this a cogent reason to ask God for the conversion of the wicked and the perseverance of the good? The reapers too are typical of the angels, who are to separate the just from the unjust.

*Resolution.* I will often pray to my own guardian angel, and to those of my parents and others, to lead many souls to heaven.

*Prayer.* Make me fervent and faithful, O my God, so that I may obtain the grace of being ranked among the good. May the just persevere, and may the wicked be converted !

## CHAPTER LXV.

### THE RETURN OF THE APOSTLES.

And the apostles coming together unto Jesus, related to him all things that they had done and taught.

And he said to them: Come apart into a desert place, and rest a little. For there were many coming and going: and they had not so much as time to eat.

And going up into a ship, they went into a desert place apart.—*St. Mark vi. 30-32.*

*Preparatory Prayer.* Help me, O my God, to be recollected, and to profit by Thy teaching.

I. Obedient to the Saviour's commands, the Apostles had gone at once to preach His coming, and at first encountered none of the difficulties which beset their subsequent labours.

They then returned to Jesus, quite elated by their first successes, and the more so, because they were barely instructed themselves. They were consequently most anxious to relate to Him every detail of their journey, and being still concerned with external things, they did not yet understand the necessity of prayer and recollection. Our Lord, therefore, said to them: "Come apart into a desert place and rest a little:" and taking them all with Him in the boat, He withdrew to a secluded spot.

II. Here again, I notice the great contrast between our Lord and His disciples. They make no effort to check their feelings of excitement, too eager, though in a good cause, while Jesus still preserves His calm and recollected demeanour.

He wishes to show that all enthusiasm, even such as theirs, requires to be kept in bounds. Probably some of the Apostles were surprised, and even showed that they did not wish their work to be thus interrupted. Yet a little reflection on the wonderful advantage of such a solitude, would have made them eager to listen to Jesus' exhortations in peace and quiet. I, too, am sometimes called upon to make a little retreat, suitable to my age. Do I make it willingly? Does my wish to profit by it, and my recollected behaviour during it, increase the grace which our Lord grants in saying to me, as to the Apostles, "Come apart and rest a little?"

*Resolution.* Henceforth in all my retreats, and even daily, at my morning and evening prayers, I will try to be recollected, and united to our Lord.

*Prayer.* O my God, since without Thy aid, I am incapable of any good action, grant that I may be always united to Thee by sanctifying grace, and the desire of doing Thy Will.

## CHAPTER LXVI.

### THE CROWD FOLLOW JESUS.

And Jesus going out saw a great multitude; and he had compassion on them, because they were as sheep not having a shepherd, and he began to teach them many things.

And when the day was now far spent, his disciples came to him, saying: This is a desert place, and the hour is now past:

Send them away, that going into the next villages and towns, they may buy themselves meat to eat.—*St. Mark vi. 34-36.*

*Preparatory Prayer.* My Saviour, deign to remove every distraction far from me.

I. Jesus, seeing a large crowd following Him, had pity on them, and began to instruct them. "And when the day was now far spent, His disciples came to him, saying: This is a desert place, and the hour is now past. Send them away, that going into the next villages and towns, they may buy themselves meat to eat. And He answering said to them: Give you them to eat."

Jesus is still the same kind and condescending Saviour. But the Apostles, once more intent on the necessaries of the material life, have not yet caught His spirit of charity, and the crowd, too, in their desire to hear Jesus, press around Him, utterly forgetful of the near approach of night, and their own fatigue and want of food. Let me profit by these different lessons.

II. I cannot fail to observe the all but want of respect for our Lord, here shown by the Apostles. He however, seemingly takes no notice of their efforts to make Him adopt their will. They tell Him to send the people away, and in this they show great indiscretion, though actuated by a good motive. How often have not I importuned my parents with questions about my small concerns, and even persisted in talking about them, whenever their indulgent kindness, no doubt in imitation of Jesus, left me unreproved!

*Resolution.* I will always try to be very respectful towards my parents and superiors, however hard it may be at times.

*Prayer.* Teach me, O my God, to keep a watch over my tongue, and grant that the remembrance of to-day's meditation may help to keep me silent, whenever I am inclined to dictate to others.

## CHAPTER LXVII.

### THE FIVE LOAVES.

And he answering said to them : Give you them to eat. And they said to him : Let us go and buy bread for two hundred pence, and we will give them to eat.

And he saith to them : How many loaves have you ? go and see. And when they knew, they say, Five, and two fishes.

And he commanded them that they should make them all sit down by companies upon the green grass.

And they sat down in ranks, by hundreds and by fifties.

And when he had taken the five loaves, and the two fishes, looking up to heaven, he blessed, and broke the loaves, and gave to his disciples to set before them : and the two fishes he divided among them all.

And they all did eat, and had their fill.—*St. Mark vi. 37-42.*

*Preparatory Prayer.* O Lord, make me understand Thy words and the lessons they teach.

I. I have already noticed how the disciples entreat Jesus to send away the crowd, and have considered our Lord's reply, "Give you them to eat." After which, they ask if they are to go and buy bread for two hundred pence, so as to feed the people. Jesus' answer is, 'How many loaves have you?' And after counting they tell Him : "Five loaves and two fishes." Thus do the disciples already feel the firm but gentle influence of their Lord. He does not reprimand, but makes them do His Will in spite of their many imperfections, for it is only after the descent of the Holy Ghost that we see them endowed with so many heroic virtues. O Jesus, how thoughtful and merciful on Thy part, thus to exert Thy authority, in order to bestow Thy fatherly gifts on the crowd that surrounded Thee!

Thou wert not content with supplying the food: Thou didst even think of the easiest way of distributing it. Probably the very selfishness of the disciples made our Lord more eager to correct any evil results that might ensue from their want of generosity. "And He commanded them that they should make them sit down by companies upon the green grass. And they sat down in ranks, by hundreds and fifties."

II. The people knew how kind Jesus was to every one, and relying on His goodness, they obeyed Him.

"And when He had taken the five loaves, and the two fishes: looking up to heaven, He blessed, and broke the loaves, and gave to His disciples to set before them: and the two fishes He divided among them all."

Thus to the astonishment of the Apostles, who, though ashamed of their selfishness, must yet have experienced a wonderful increase of confidence, did our Lord supply and distribute food to the multitude. Let me, like the Apostles, revive my trust in God, as I contemplate this miracle.

*Resolution.* I will confide everything to Almighty God, family affairs, the commands of my parents, health and sickness, for I know that He ordains all things. Especially in time of trial will I submit to Divine Providence.

*Prayer.* O Lord, teach me to make frequent acts of submission to whatever Thou decree'st in my regard.

## CHAPTER LXVIII.

### THE TWELVE BASKETS.

And when they were filled, he said to his disciples: Gather up the fragments that remain, lest they be lost.

They gathered up therefore, and filled twelve baskets with the fragments of the five barley loaves, which remained over and above to them that had eaten.

Now those men, when they had seen what a miracle Jesus had done, said: This is of a truth the prophet that is to come into the world.—*St. John vi. 12-14.*

*Preparatory Prayer.* Help me, O my God, to study even Thy smallest actions, and show me how to draw profit from them.

I. After relating the miracle of the loaves and fishes, the holy Gospel tells us that "they all did eat, and had their fill."

Wonder and gratitude must have been uppermost in the minds of all present, and doubtless all were ready to acknowledge the Saviour. Before, however, the people return to their homes, Jesus, wishing to teach His disciples never to neglect even small duties, says to them in the words of the Evangelist, "*Gather up the fragments that remain, lest they be lost.* They gathered up therefore, and filled twelve baskets with the fragments of the five barley loaves, which remained over and above to them that had eaten."

The crowd helped the disciples, and all wondered at the immense quantity that was left.

II. Our Lord, Who in all His life never worked a miracle for His own comfort, but lived in the simplest and poorest way possible, most probably only supped Himself after the crowd had dispersed, and then off these very fragments. O my God, what a beautiful sight to see Thee satisfied with what the poor had left! I cannot help recognising that it is for me that Jesus thus deprives Himself. I will profit by this wonderful lesson of order and sobriety, and henceforth resolve never to waste anything. Indeed, if I but considered the poor, such a custom would become easy. When there are so many who, though they work hard, are unable to feed themselves or their children, is it not wrong to waste what they might eat?

*Resolution.* In future I will never waste anything, not even bread, nor leave an unfinished piece because I see something else which I prefer.

*Prayer.* Thou givest me, O my God, abundantly of everything I need: make me ever use Thy gifts in moderation and with gratitude.

## CHAPTER LXIX.

### JESUS WALKING ON THE WATER.

And forthwith Jesus obliged his disciples to go up into the boat, and to go before him over the water, till he dismissed the multitudes.

And having dismissed the multitude, he went up into a mountain alone to pray. And when it was evening, he was there alone.

But the boat in the midst of the sea was tossed with the waves: for the wind was contrary.

And in the fourth watch of the night, he came to them walking upon the sea.

And they seeing him walking upon the sea, were troubled, saying: It is an apparition. And they cried out for fear.

And immediately Jesus spoke to them, saying: Be of good heart: It is I, fear ye not.—*St. Matthew xiv. 22-27.*

*Preparatory Prayer.* O Lord, deign to speak to me, humbly prostrate at Thy Feet.

I. Jesus, before returning to the mountain to pray in solitude, had told His disciples to enter their boat and cross the lake alone. The wind was, however, contrary, and they had to struggle as best they could in their storm-tossed bark. Our Lord, no doubt out of pity, shortened His prayer, so as to hasten to their assistance. Nothing is impossible to Almighty God, so "He came to them walking upon the sea. And they seeing Him walking upon the sea were troubled, saying: It is an apparition. And they cried out for fear." Why had they not greater confidence in Jesus, in obedience to Whose command they had already seen the wind and storm cease? Still they were afraid, so Jesus said to them, "Be of good heart: it is I, fear ye not." Yes, dear Lord, even hadst Thou not said it, I should have recognised Thee by the paternal care with which Thou didst comfort Thy Apostles in their hour of need. I behold them troubled and in want of help, whilst Thou, O Lord, without blaming their weakness, comest to encourage them and dispel their fear.

II. In the same way, and in every age, does Jesus in the Blessed Sacrament come to those that fear, no matter what be the subject of their dread, and, making known His mercy, say to all, "Be of good heart: it is I, fear ye not." When death approaches, He is our consolation. He sends to our sick-bed the priest, the nun, or pious relatives who, one and all, tell us in His Name not to fear; and finally He comes Himself in the Viaticum, and once more repeats, "Be of good heart, it is I, fear ye not." But notwithstanding the peace and tranquillity that religion brings to the dying, how often do not those around a departing friend almost fear to speak of God or confession! What a misfortune! Have I not seen that Jesus can calm the winds and waves, and therefore should I not rely on Him by His Blessed Presence, and Holy Sacraments, to smooth away all difficulties, prepare the dying, and bring them peace and comfort?

*Resolution.* Henceforth, whenever occasion arises, I will not fail to speak to the dying of the last Sacraments. May our Lord help me to keep my good resolution.

*Prayer.* Dear Lord, vouchsafe to visit me when my soul is troubled and afraid. Oh, come to me especially at my last hour, and grant this grace to all who are in their agony!

# CHAPTER LXX.

## LORD, SAVE ME!

And Peter making answer, said : Lord, if it be thou, bid me come to thee upon the waters.

And he said : Come. And Peter going down out of the boat, walked upon the water to come to Jesus.

But seeing the wind strong, he was afraid : and when he began to sink, he cried out, saying : Lord, save me.

And immediately Jesus stretching forth his hand took hold of him, and said to him : O thou of little faith, why didst thou doubt ?

And when they were come up into the boat, the wind ceased.

And they that were in the boat came and adored him, saying : Indeed thou art the Son of God.—*St. Matthew xiv. 28-33.*

*Preparatory Prayer.* I desire, O my God, to study and imitate Thy adorable example : do Thou help me.

I. I have seen how our Lord came and spoke to the Apostles in their boat. But St. Peter being still afraid cried out, "Lord, if it be Thou, bid me come to Thee on the waters. And He said : Come. And Peter going down out of the boat, walked upon the water to come to Jesus." St. Peter, though always anxious and ready to believe and love, nevertheless once again yields too easily to fear at the first appearance of danger. Without thinking of what he is doing, he gets out of the boat, while his companions look on with dread. Everything around them wears a fearful aspect. The waves beat wildly against the boat, yet our Lord, in the very centre of the storm, walks calmly on the water. The confidence, inspired by His words, does not, however, long sustain St. Peter's failing courage. "But seeing the wind strong, he was afraid: and when he began to sink, he cried out saying: Lord, save me. And immediately Jesus stretching forth His Hand took hold of him, and said to him: O thou of little faith, why didst thou doubt?"

II. Our Lord acts similarly, every day, with the willing soul, when, drawn by an irresistible impulse towards a more perfect life, God's call alone seems necessary to enable her to walk on the troubled waters, or, in other words, to overcome her inclinations and temptations. In her eager transports, she cries out to our Lord, "Tell me to come to Thee." But scarcely has she set out on her way, that is, begun to correct her faults, than she is discouraged, and in her fear calls upon Jesus to save her. Our Lord, never deaf to such an appeal, stretches forth His saving Hand in mercy.

*Resolution.* Whenever I see the necessity of correcting my faults of character or the like, I will endeavour to make the effort which Almighty God requires of me, and with His help I will persevere therein, never losing courage. The moment, too, that I feel my strength fail, I will cry out with St. Peter, "Lord, save me."

*Prayer.* O Jesus, make me always turn to Thee, no matter how I may be circumstanced!

## CHAPTER LXXI.

### TO WHOM SHALL WE GO?

After this many of his disciples went back; and walked no more with him.

Then Jesus said to the twelve: Will you also go away?

And Simon Peter answered him: Lord, to whom shall we go? thou hast the words of eternal life.

And we have believed and have known that thou art the Christ the Son of God.—*St. John vi. 67-70.*

*Preparatory Prayer.* O Jesus, make me love, obey and follow Thee!

I. It is universally admitted that the miracle of the loaves was a figure of the Blessed Eucharist. Indeed, the miraculous food which our Lord gave to the exhausted multitude, was clearly a picture of the supernatural nourishment that Jesus gives us when we receive His very Self in Holy Communion. Poor weary travellers are we, and worn out as we journey on through life. Jesus makes us rest a little; and out of pity for our weakness, and in order to enable us to reach our destination, He deigns to give us Himself for our food. In every age and in every part of the world He multiplies His Adorable Body by a miracle, as stupendous, and yet for Him as easy, as that by which five loaves and two fishes were more than enough to feed five thousand people.

II. As the Gospel tells us, after Jesus had returned to Capharnaum, wishing, no doubt, to profit by the impression caused by this wonderful miracle, He spoke to the Jews of the Holy Eucharist, but they did not understand Him, and even, to quote the words of the Evangelist, "many of His disciples went back, and walked no more with Him. Then Jesus said to the twelve: Will you also go away? And Simon Peter answered Him: Lord, to whom shall we go? Thou hast the words of eternal life."

I can imagine St. Peter throwing himself before our Lord, as He says this, while, looking at Him tenderly, he protests his love and confidence as much by his respectful and filial manner, as by his words. This sublime act of faith on the part of St. Peter ought to serve as a model for me, both with regard to the holy mysteries of our religion, as well as everything that Divine Providence ordains on my behalf. Probably I shall at times be tempted: things will appear too difficult to do or to believe. What shall I then do, but throw myself at Jesus' Feet, and silence reason, that I may listen to the voice of faith which speaks to the heart, and repeat with St. Peter, "To whom shall we go? Thou hast the words of eternal life."

*Resolution.* I will often repeat these very words, so that they may become familiar to me, and rise to my lips, without effort, in time of temptation.

*Prayer.* O Jesus, Thou Who art the Way, the Truth, and the Light, make me always follow Thee, no matter how difficult the road may appear.

## CHAPTER LXXII.

### THE WOMAN OF CANAAN.

And Jesus went from thence, and retired into the coasts of Tyre and Sidon.

And behold a woman of Canaan who came out, said to him: Have mercy on me, O Lord, thou son of David: my daughter is grievously troubled by a devil.

Who answered her not a word. And his disciples came and besought him, saying: Send her away, for she crieth after us.

And he answering, said: I was not sent but to the sheep that are lost of the house of Israel.

But she came and adored him, saying: Lord, help me.

Who answering, said: It is not good to take the bread of the children, and to cast it to the dogs.

But she said: Yea, Lord, for the whelps also eat of the crumbs that fall from the table of their masters.

Then Jesus answering said to her: O woman, great is thy faith: be it done to thee as thou wilt: and her daughter was cured from that hour.—*St. Matthew xv. 21-28.*

*Preparatory Prayer.* My good Master, behold me at Thy Feet, make me attentive, and deign to instruct me Thyself.

I. Jesus having come, in the course of His preaching, near Tyre and Sidon, a Canaanite woman thus addressed Him, "Have mercy on me, O Lord, Thou Son of David, my daughter is grievously tormented by a devil."

Our Lord did not reply, either because she was a pagan, or to give us a lesson of humility.

She, however, continued to cry out more loudly, so that the disciples besought our Lord to send her away. Still Jesus, Who is generally so kind to those in suffering and so ready to comfort them, does not yield, and, with seeming indifference, replies: " I was not sent but to the sheep that are lost of the house of Israel," that is to say, why should I trouble about any other but the true fold? The poor woman is, however, a mother, and, in her desire to obtain her daughter's cure, she does not recoil. "But she came and adored Him, saying: Lord, help me." Jesus, knowing what she wanted, nevertheless replied : " It is not good to take the bread of the children and to cast it to the dogs."

II. It seems hard, at first, to understand why such a good and tender Master should have made so severe a reply. The poor woman, overcome, bursts into tears. And I know how deeply Jesus must have suffered thus to prolong the agony of a mother asking her daughter's cure: but He wished her humility to be made known. The poor woman replied : " Yea, Lord, for the whelps also eat of the crumbs that fall from the table of their masters." And in answer Jesus cried out: "O woman, great is thy faith, be it done to thee as thou wilt : and her daughter was cured from that hour."

This poor Canaanite has come down to us through many ages, as an example of humble, persevering confidence. God refuses nothing to prayer such as hers.

*Resolution.* I will never murmur or shew discontent, when my prayers seem unheard, but remember that increased humility is the best means to obtain what I want.

*Prayer.* O Lord, deign to hear my prayer, which I will often repeat, 'Make me humble and tender of heart.'

## CHAPTER LXXIII.

### THE DEAF AND DUMB MAN.

And they bring to him one deaf and dumb: and they besought him that he would lay his hand upon him.

And taking him from the multitude apart, he put his fingers into his ears, and spitting, he touched his tongue:

And looking up to heaven, he groaned, and said to him: Ephpheta, which is, Be thou opened.

And immediately his ears were opened, and the string of his tongue was loosed, and he spoke right.

And he charged them that they should tell no man. But the more he charged them, so much the more a great deal did they publish it.

And so much the more did they wonder, saying: He hath done all things well: he hath made both the deaf to hear, and the dumb to speak.—*St. Mark vii. 32-37.*

*Preparatory Prayer.* My good Master, help me to understand Thy teaching, and to profit by it.

I. As our Lord, after leaving Tyre, passed by Sidon towards the sea of Galilee, the people brought Him one deaf and dumb, and besought Him to lay His Hands upon him, and cure him: for it was thus that Jesus was accustomed to work His greatest miracles. Almighty God, however, though He condescends to hear the prayers, which He desires us to address to Him, frequently grants our requests in His own measure and way. And here, perhaps better to make us realise His Omnipotence, He acts in a different manner, for, "taking him from the multitude apart, He put His fingers into his ears, and spitting, He touched his tongue: And looking up to heaven, He groaned, and said to him: Ephpheta, which is, Be thou opened. And immediately his ears were opened, and the string of his tongue was loosed, and he spoke right."

II. Let me observe the tender care which Jesus lavishes on this poor man. His Divine Countenance seems to beam with greater compassion than usual. He is touched with pity at the sight of such misery, and draws the poor man close to Him, as though to bless him in an especial manner, while a sigh shows still more plainly what is passing in His Sacred Heart. On the other hand, the object of His compassion stands there before his Lord, watching His every movement. Even though he has not heard the people's prayer for his cure, his heart beats quick with the desire to be healed, and he is ready to do whatever Jesus may command, as he waits and hopes. What then must have been his joy to hear the Saviour say, "Ephpheta," and to feel his tongue loosened on the instant? Surely his first speech must have been one of earnest thanks to God! What endless graces has not Jesus bestowed on me during the course of my life! He has preserved me and those dear to me, and given me all I stand in need of! Thanksgiving then, which, Saints tell us, is the best of prayers, should be my constant practice.

*Resolution.* I will try to render my life one continual act of thanksgiving to God, and more particularly, whenever He grants me any special grace either spiritual or temporal.

*Prayer.* My God, I live by Thy gifts, grant me the grace to lead a life of thanksgiving.

## CHAPTER LXXIV.

### THE BLIND MAN OF BETHSAIDA.

And they came to Bethsaida, and they bring to him a blind man, and they besought him that he would touch him.

And taking the blind man by the hand he led him out of the town: and spitting upon his eyes, laying his hands on him, he asked him if he saw anything.—*St. Mark viii. 22, 23.*

*Preparatory Prayer.* Lord Jesus, I beg of Thee, make me attentive and recollected.

I. As the Holy Gospel tells us, there was a poor blind man at Bethsaida, whom the people led to Jesus, so that He might cure him. I will meditate on the kindness and goodness of our Lord, when the blind man is brought to Him. At once approaching, He takes him by the hand and leads him gently out of the town. Jesus' Countenance is grave but full of tender mercy, while the object of His compassion, astonished and moved at the thought of being cured, offers no resistance. O Jesus, grant me ever so to act. How often indeed hast Thou taken me by the hand and led me apart, by inspiring me with good thoughts or generous resolutions, and alas! how often have I not resisted Thy divine guidance? What would the disciples have said, had the blind man acted thus and turned his back on Jesus? But what else do I do, whenever I either deliberately, or by carelessness or childishness reject God's good inspirations, but turn my back on our Lord and refuse His holy light?

II. Jesus, continues the Gospel, "spitting upon his eyes, and laying His hands on him, asked him if he saw anything."

I will here pause for a moment to observe what our Lord does. I know He was powerful enough to cure the blind, without any external signs, just as he merely said to the paralytic, "Take up thy bed and walk." But in this case we have an important lesson to learn. Jesus wished to teach us how great should be our respect for the ritual of the Church in the administration of the Sacraments, where everything is done so simply and yet so grandly.

*Resolution.* If my ignorance prevents me from understanding the symbolical meaning of all the priest does at the altar, I will, at least, respect, and let my behaviour show that I respect, even the smallest detail of the Church's ceremonies.

*Prayer.* My God, pardon the inattention with which I have hitherto assisted at religious functions, and deign to make me understand their deep meaning.

## CHAPTER LXXV.

### THE BLIND MAN OF BETHSAIDA.—*Continued.*

And looking up, he said : I see men as it were trees, walking. After that again he laid his hands upon his eyes, and he began to see, and was restored, so that he saw all things clearly. —*St. Mark viii. 24, 25.*

*Preparatory Prayer.* Lord, make me understand Thy divine teaching.

I. I have seen that, after our Lord touched the eyes of the blind man, He asked him if he saw anything. "I see men as it were trees, walking," was the reply. Although he saw, his vision was still confused. "After that again He laid His hands upon his eyes, and he began to see, and was restored, so that he saw all things clearly." Here, then, do I find another practical lesson. When I desire to overcome a failing or evil inclination, such as laziness, pride or what not, I have already received a grace, viz., the consciousness that there is something for me to remedy. At this stage, and until I know how to set about my cure, I am like the blind man of Bethsaida who "saw men as it were trees, walking." I am as yet unable to see distinctly, and I do not understand what I have to do to correct my fault.

At such a time, therefore, instead of being cast

down by my own powerlessness, I should reflect that Almighty God, Who has already begun my cure, will, no doubt, in His goodness complete it, and will, by touching my eyes a second time, enable me to see not only the obstacle, but the means necessary to overcome it. O my God, teach me always to rely on Thy divine goodness, even though Thou may'st delay Thy merciful aid.

II. Jesus, after having proved that the man saw, dismissed him, saying: "Go into thy house and if thou enter into the town, tell nobody." The Gospel does not explain why our Lord here enjoined silence: this command of His should, however, teach me the advantage of discretion.

I must learn to restrain myself, and not impart my feelings to everyone, even when my heart is full of any emotion, or my mind the prey to an all-absorbing thought. I must never repeat what I am told in confidence, nor unnecessarily speak of any good I may happen to do.

*Resolution.* I will try stedfastly to curb my dominant passion, and never allow myself to be discouraged. Whenever I fall, I will ask our Lord to touch me once again, that I may be completely cured.

*Prayer.* O God, keep a watch over my mouth, and restrain me whenever I am tempted to speak in an indiscreet manner.

## CHAPTER LXXVI.

### THOU ART THE CHRIST.

And Jesus went out, and his disciples, into the towns of Cæsarea-Philippi ; and in the way he asked his disciples, saying to them : Whom do men say that I am ?

Who answered him, saying : John the Baptist ; but some Elias, and others as one of the prophets.

Then he saith to them : But whom do you say that I am ? Peter answering said to him : Thou art the Christ.

And he strictly charged them that they should not tell any man of him.—*St. Mark viii. 27-30.*

*Preparatory Prayer.* Dear Lord, behold me at Thy Feet, ready to listen to Thy teachings. Oh, make me understand them !

I. Jesus, in curing the blind man at Bethsaida, had just given another proof that He was the Son of God; yet, knowing how reluctant some men are to believe even what they see, He gave His disciples a further opportunity of showing their faith in His Divinity, by asking them, as He proceeded along the road from Bethsaida, "Whom do men say that I am ?"

My good Master, how sweet and familiar was the intimacy between Thee and Thy disciples! What simplicity and kindness in Thy very questions! What confidence and love must they have had in and for Thee! Yet Thou art still the same Jesus; and therefore I ought always to receive Thee in Holy Communion with the same spirit, and speak my thoughts and wishes openly to Thee. Oh, would that I could understand this holy union with God, and hear and answer His questions! Would that I knew how to converse with Jesus and make the same use of my conversation as did St. Peter!

II. The disciples answered our Lord's question, according to what they had heard, and Jesus then, more pointedly, said to them: "But whom do you say that I am?" St. Peter answered and said: "Thou art the Christ."

No doubt, at this reply, the other disciples remained silent, acquiescing in St. Peter's act of faith. "Thou art the Christ," should also be my cry, whenever I have need of help, and feel myself weak in the service of God. Of myself, I am incapable of any good, but if I say to Jesus, "Thou art the Christ," that is, I believe in and adore Thee, and acknowledge Thy supreme rule over me, if I repeat St. Peter's act of affirmation with all my heart, I am sure that God will deign to help me with His holy grace.

*Resolution.* I will constantly ask of Jesus a lively and solid faith, and will always try in my prayers to say my act of faith with the greatest attention.

*Prayer.* My God, make me frequently repeat these words, 'I believe, but do Thou increase my faith,' and deign, O Lord, to hear my prayer.

# CHAPTER LXXVII.

## BLESSED ART THOU, SIMON BAR-JONA.

Simon Peter answered and said: Thou art Christ the Son of the living God.

And Jesus answering, said to him: Blessed art thou, Simon Bar-jona: because flesh and blood hath not revealed it to thee, but my Father who is in heaven.

And I say to thee: That thou art Peter; and upon this rock I will build my church, and the gates of hell shall not prevail against it.

And I will give to thee the keys of the kingdom of heaven. And whatsoever thou shalt bind upon earth, it shall be bound also in heaven: and whatsoever thou shalt loose on earth, it shall be loosed also in heaven.—*St. Matthew xvi. 16-19.*

*Preparatory Prayer.* My God, behold me in spirit at Thy Feet in company with Thy Apostles: deign to instruct me also in the same manner.

I. Having heard St. Peter exclaim, "Thou art the Christ," let me consider our Lord's reply, "Blessed art thou, Simon Bar-Jona: because flesh and blood hath not revealed it to thee but My Father Who is in heaven. And I say to thee: That thou art Peter; and upon this rock will I build My Church, and the gates of hell shall not prevail against it." How solemn must have been Jesus' manner, when He thus divinely prophesied the establishment of the Universal Church, and promised that she should never fail, but should last to the end of time. St. Peter, the poor fisherman, whom Jesus had promised to make a fisher of men, is then the rock on which the Church of God rests. She is therefore often called the Bark of Peter, and in her course, though frequently tossed about by the waves, she always weathers the storm, bringing salvation to every generation.

II. Let these words of Jesus to St. Peter revive my faith. The assurance that hell shall never overthrow the Church, should give us the greatest confidence, even when she is assailed by the most terrible assaults of the devil. History shows that Satan has never ceased to wage furious war against all the Popes, who are St. Peter's successors, and yet for more than 1800 years, and despite the greatest obstacles, they have succeeded one another without interruption, and have never ceased to govern the flock of Christ.

Yet, while my faith should be strong and lively, I must not forget that God wishes us to pray, and to ask for the graces with which He desires to endow us, and so, notwithstanding Christ's assurance, it is still my duty to pray for the welfare of the Church. What real happiness it is for the true Christian to visit Rome and St. Peter's prison, to venerate the chains with which the Apostle was bound, and to assist at Mass at his tomb, which, from its position beneath the Basilica, suggests the idea of a foundation stone, and is typical of the rock on which Christ built His ever-enduring

Church! How easy must it be in that holy spot to be recollected and pray for the Church, but the thought of what a blessing it is to be a Catholic, should everywhere re-enkindle my filial devotion.

*Resolution.* From this day forward, I will add to my prayers the invocation, "SS. Peter and Paul, pray for the holy Church."

*Prayer.* O God, Who by a special grace hast made me a Catholic and Thy child, grant that Thy kingdom may come and Thy Church extend over all the earth.

## CHAPTER LXXVIII.

### JESUS FORETELLS HIS SUFFERINGS.

From that time Jesus began to show to his disciples, that he must go to Jerusalem, and suffer many things from the ancients and scribes and chief-priests, and be put to death, and the third day rise again.

And Peter taking him, began to rebuke him, saying: Lord, be it far from thee, this shall not be unto thee.

Who turning said to Peter: Go behind me, satan, thou art a scandal unto me: because thou savourest not the things that are of God, but the things that are of men.

Then Jesus said to his disciples: If any man will come after me, let him deny himself, and take up his cross and follow me.
—*St. Matthew xvi. 21-24.*

*Preparatory Prayer.* My God, do Thou Thyself deign to speak to my heart, so that I may ever love Thee more and more.

I. Our Lord did not speak to the Apostles of His Passion, till he had encouraged and strengthened them by the promise of an infallible Church. He wished them, no doubt, to be strong in confidence before having to contemplate the dark perspective. But, immediately after He had assured them that the gates of hell should not prevail against His Church, Jesus tells them that He must suffer much Himself, and be condemned to death, but that He will rise again on the third day. This news saddens the Apostles, although they do not rightly understand all the humiliations and tortures that Jesus tells them are in store for Him. Neither His teachings, His grave discourses, nor the self-denial He makes them practise, have as yet affected their inmost hearts. Later, after the descent of the Holy Ghost, they will generously embrace a life of suffering, but at present they are still imperfect, and cannot understand that their Master should be subjected to contumely and insults.

They therefore remain silent and thoughtful, hardly daring to confess their repugnance, yet their looks betray them.

II. St. Peter, who was already marked out as their chief, and the foundation-stone of the Church, being eager to prove his love for our Lord, could not restrain himself, but according to the Gospel, "taking Jesus, began to rebuke Him, saying: Lord be it far from Thee, this shall not be unto Thee."

Let me observe the contrast between the animated appearance and indignation of the Apostle, and Jesus' calm demeanour. Scarcely had St. Peter spoken, than our Lord ordered him to be silent: "Go behind Me, Satan, thou art a scandal unto Me: because thou savourest not the things that are of God, but the things that are of men."

The Apostle must, at first, have been saddened at being thus repulsed by our Lord, usually so tender towards him. But Jesus continued: "If any man will come after Me, let him deny himself, and take up his cross and follow Me:" and then St. Peter understood that our Lord's Passion, as foretold by Himself, was to be the great example to teach and strengthen mankind. He felt that to follow Jesus was to take up the cross, and therefore he was silent.

*Resolution.* I know that I too, if I am to be Jesus' disciple, must carry the cross. In His goodness, He will regulate it according to my strength. I will not, then, be afraid, but will accept beforehand whatever trials Almighty God is pleased to send me, and will begin to-day to bear all my crosses with patience.

*Prayer.* O Jesus, I wish ever to follow Thee. Grant me the grace to renounce generously whatever is displeasing to Thee, so that I may walk closely in Thy footsteps.

## CHAPTER LXXIX.

### THE TRANSFIGURATION.

And it came to pass about eight days after these words, that he took Peter and James and John, and went up into a mountain to pray.

And whilst he prayed, the shape of his countenance was altered, and his raiment became white and glittering,

And behold two men were talking with him. And they were Moses and Elias,

Appearing in majesty. And they spoke of his decease that he should accomplish in Jerusalem.

But Peter and they that were with him, were heavy with sleep. And waking, they saw his glory, and the two men that stood with him.—*St. Luke ix. 28-32.*

*Preparatory Prayer.* My Good Master, make me always recollected in Thy divine presence.

I. "Jesus took Peter and James and John, and went up into a mountain to pray." These three disciples were also subsequently to accompany their Master to the Garden of Olives. Jesus did not explain why it was that He chose them now, but holy writers say that, as they were to be present at His agony, our Lord wished previously to fortify them, by the sight of His glory.

The three disciples, then, obeying Jesus' call, journey

along the rough path, which leads to the summit of the mountain: but they follow without any enthusiasm and even, as the Gospel tells us, are overcome by sleep. Perhaps also, they inwardly grumbled that our Lord should take them with Him to pray, when they needed rest; and yet I shall see directly how great was their privilege.

Ought not this to make me understand that every trial, rightly accepted, nearly always brings with it its own reward? It is worth while, then, to make every effort to overcome such difficulties as may lie in the way of God's grace.

II. When they reached the top of the mountain, they all knelt down; "and whilst Jesus prayed, the shape of His Countenance was altered, and his raiment became white and glittering." Let me try to see what the three disciples saw.

The splendour and majesty of Jesus' Face, though, as ever, all sweetness, is so great, its brightness so intense, that I am as completely dazzled, as if I had suddenly been transported from the darkness of night into the strongest sunshine.

My God, permit me to gaze upon Thee, without being blinded. How beautiful Thou art, and how brilliant the light of Thy glory! Still I am not afraid, for Thou art ever my Saviour and kind Master. As I look again, Thou art no longer alone: Moses and Elias are with Thee, and, as though to show me that Thou art really my Redeemer, they speak with Thee of Thy

Passion and Death, which were to obtain for me my salvation.

Thy Omnipotence, then, does not even save Thee from suffering and dying for me! Surely the thought of Thy great humiliation, O God of glory, should make me willingly bear all the little mortifications of my daily life!

*Resolution.* In future, from this very day, I will restrain every feeling of jealousy and ill-will towards my more favoured companions.

*Prayer.* O Jesus, Who in Thy glory makest me think of Thy sufferings, grant me the grace to bear with patience whatever wounds my self-love.

## CHAPTER LXXX.

### THE THREE TABERNACLES.

Peter saith to Jesus: Master, it is good for us to be here: and let us make three tabernacles, one for thee, and one for Moses, and one for Elias: not knowing what he said.

And as he spoke these things, there came a cloud, and overshadowed them: and they were afraid, when they entered into the cloud.

And a voice came out of the cloud saying: This is my beloved Son, hear him.

And whilst the voice was uttered, Jesus was found alone. — *St. Luke ix. 33-36.*

*Preparatory Prayer.* I am still present in spirit at Thy Transfiguration, O Jesus; permit me to remain there with Thy disciples.

I. Before leaving Mount Thabor, let me hear what St. Peter says: "Master, it is good for us to be here; and let us make three tabernacles, one for Thee, and one for Moses, and one for Elias."

St. Peter and his two companions hardly know where they are, or what they are doing. They are completely lost in admiration, and their only wish is to stay where they are partakers, as it were, of so much glory. Alas, the first motion of the human heart, when satisfied, is one of selfishness and personal gratification.

The disciples, though they hear Moses and Elias speak of Jesus' death, endeavour not to think of it. Despite all that our Lord has already taught them, they prefer glory to opprobrium. 'It is good for us to be here.' Have not I, alas! too often said, I will stay wherever I am comfortable, and speedily retreat from whatever troubles and disturbs me? Is it not precisely this, that the devil whispers in my ear, when, instead of hurrying to my studies, or other unpleasant duties, I lose my time in recreation?

II. "And as he spoke these things, there came a cloud, and overshadowed them: and they were afraid, when they entered into the cloud." Thus, all of a sudden, the dazzling brightness is hidden from them, and the mountain is wrapt in darkness. What a change! The disciples are seized with fear. But Thou wishest to teach me, O Jesus, how all that dazzles in this world is but as a passing shadow. "And a voice came out of the cloud saying: *This is My beloved Son, hear Him.* And whilst the voice was uttered, Jesus was found alone."

O Jesus, Thou art once more my own sweet Saviour, humble and bereft of Thy majesty as before Thy Transfiguration. Nevertheless, I have heard the divine voice tell me, that Thou art the well-beloved Son of God, the Creator of all things, and I can no more doubt that Thou art my Lord and Master, than when Thou wert resplendent in all Thy glory. Thou here teachest me how little regard I should have for external appearances.

*Resolution.* I will carefully be on my guard against being carried away by all outward show, such as elegance, riches and the like, remembering that all these add no merit in the sight of God.

*Prayer.* O God, Who lookest only to the heart, enrich mine, and clothe it with whatever is pleasing to Thee.

# CHAPTER LXXXI.

### JESUS DESCENDS FROM THE MOUNTAIN.

And immediately looking about, they saw no man any more but Jesus only with them.

And as they came down from the mountain, he charged them not to tell any man what things they had seen, till the Son of man shall be risen again from the dead.

And they kept the word to themselves; questioning together what that should mean, When he shall be risen from the dead. —*St. Mark ix. 7-9.*

*Preparatory Prayer.* My Saviour, I desire to listen to Thee, deign to penetrate my heart with Thy divine teaching.

I. After the Transfiguration, and when the voice in the cloud had ceased, Jesus, with perfect calmness, commences to descend the path that leads down the mountain. His disciples, however, are still much impressed by what they have just witnessed, and are, as it were, dazed. They look at our Lord, Whom they follow in silence, not yet daring to question Him. Let me, too, follow Jesus, and be attentive to what He says. "And as they came down from the mountain, He charged them not to tell any man what things they had seen, till the Son of man shall be risen again from the dead." The disciples did as Jesus commanded, but, as the Gospel tells us, "questioning together what that should mean: when He shall be risen from the dead."

This shows how little they as yet understood all that our Lord had foretold them of His Passion, Death and Resurrection.

Still Jesus, without being angry at their slowness of comprehension, does not reprove them, and is satisfied with their blind obedience in following Him and hearkening to His words.

II. Let me learn a practical lesson from this meditation.

Jesus is God, and therefore is to be obeyed. He governs the Church on earth by means of the Pope, who is His representative; and, in like manner, the Bishops and Priests transmit to all Christians the teachings of Christ's Vicar. I must therefore listen to and obey, without trying to understand, what is above my powers of comprehension. Such was the blind obedience of the Apostles on their way down from Mount Thabor. Later, they laid down their lives to bear witness to the doctrine of Christ, but at the time of the Transfiguration they contented themselves with obeying in silence. Though I am probably not called to confess the faith in persecution and martyrdom, I shall frequently, when I grow older, meet with persons, who barely recognise the authority of the Church. May I then never fail to show them an example of blind and filial submission to the Church and the Pope.

*Resolution.* I will at once begin to try and strengthen this feeling in myself, by always saying the Creed at Mass and in my prayers, with great recollectedness, endeavouring thoroughly to understand the meaning of each article.

*Prayer.* O my God, Who art truth itself, increase and strengthen my faith!

## CHAPTER LXXXII.

### THE DUMB SPIRIT.

And one of the multitude answering, said: Master, I have brought my son to thee having a dumb spirit.

Who, wheresoever he taketh him, dasheth him and he foameth, and gnasheth with the teeth, and pineth away: and I spoke to thy disciples to cast him out, and they could not.

Who answering them said: O incredulous generation, how long shall I be with you? how long shall I suffer you? bring him unto me.

And they brought him. And when he had seen him, immediately the spirit troubled him; and being thrown down upon the ground, he rolled about foaming.

And he asked his father: How long time is it since this hath happened unto him? But he said: From his infancy.

And often times hath he cast him into the fire and into waters to destroy him. But if thou canst do any thing, help us, having compassion on us.

And Jesus saith to him: If thou canst believe, all things are possible to him that believeth.

And immediately the father of the boy, crying out, with tears said: I do believe, Lord: help my unbelief.—*St. Mark ix. 16-23.*

*Preparatory Prayer.* Lord Jesus, make me know Thee and love Thee with all my heart.

I. Scarcely has Jesus come down from Mount Thabor with SS. Peter, James and John, than I see a man approach Him, saying: "Master, I have brought my son to Thee having a dumb spirit. I spoke to Thy disciples to cast him out, and they could not." Jesus answering, ordered the child to be brought to Him. "And when He had seen him immediately the spirit troubled him; and being thrown down upon the ground, he rolled about foaming." What a scene! The poor father gave way to his grief, and the crowd looked on in awe and silence, while Jesus, preserving His calm demeanour, though the boy was in a paroxysm at His Feet, asked the father: "How long time is it since this hath happened unto him? But he said: From his infancy. And often times hath he cast him into the fire, and into waters to destroy him. But if Thou canst do any thing, help us, having compassion on us."

II. Why should our Lord ask these questions, since He can read in the bottom of our hearts, and directs all things? He is more intimately acquainted with the details concerning the boy, than is his own father. He does not, however, wish to lose this opportunity of instructing the Jews and future generations of men, and myself amongst the number, and once again in His goodness desires to reveal His Omnipotence. Knowing that many an unbeliever, or critic, will try to diminish the greatness of the miracle, by saying that the disease was only of a passing nature, our Lord wishes the crowd to hear the truth, and so He goes on to say: "If thou canst believe, all things are possible to him that believeth. And immediately the father of the boy crying out, with tears said: I do believe, Lord, help my unbelief."

When I consider how this poor man, in his emotion, feared that his faith was not sufficiently great to obtain the cure of his son, what must I think of my own? Is not my want of confidence the cause of the ill success attending my prayers? When I beg a grace of God, can I say that my faith is sufficiently lively to merit that my prayer should be heard?

*Resolution.* I will at once resolve to imitate the poor boy's father, and to repeat often, especially when before the Blessed Sacrament: "I believe, O God, but do Thou increase my faith."

*Prayer.* O Lord, Who hast said, "If thou canst believe, all things are possible to him that believeth," give me, I beg of Thee, the faith that obtains everything.

## CHAPTER LXXXIII.

### JESUS CASTETH OUT THE DUMB SPIRIT.

And when Jesus saw the multitude running together, he threatened the unclean spirit, saying to him: Deaf and dumb spirit, I command thee, go out of him: and enter not any more into him.

And crying out, and greatly tearing him, he went out of him, and he became as dead, so that many said: He is dead.

But Jesus taking him by the hand, lifted him up: and he arose.

And when he was come into the house his disciples secretly asked him: Why could not we cast him out?

And he said to them: This kind can go out by nothing, but by prayer and fasting.—*St. Mark ix. 24-28.*

*Preparatory Prayer.* Behold me at Thy Feet, my Lord and Master, do Thou Thyself teach me, I beg of Thee.

I. I am once more, in spirit, in the presence of Jesus, as He questions the father of the possessed boy, who is rolling on the ground before them. "And when Jesus saw the multitude running together, He threatened the unclean spirit, saying to him: Deaf and dumb spirit, I command thee, go out of him: and enter not any more into him. And crying out, and greatly tearing him, he went out of him, and he became as dead, so that many said: He is dead. But Jesus taking him by the hand, lifted him up: and he arose. And when He was come into the house, His disciples secretly asked Him: Why could not we cast him out?" They had tried to do so, for the boy's father told our Lord that they could not. Still they had worked many other miracles in Jesus' Name, and therefore, they were anxious to know why this devil had been able to resist them successfully. Our Lord answers them with the greatest freedom, for they are now alone. I will watch and listen attentively, so that I may profit by the Saviour's reply.

II. "This kind can go out by nothing, but by prayer and fasting." This was to show the disciples that a life of prayer and penance, such as our Lord's, is often necessary to appease God's wrath, and lessen the power which He, at times, allows the devil to exercise over individuals.

This reply of Jesus, establishing the necessity of prayer and fasting, should teach me the greatest respect for those contemplative religious orders in which the monks' lives are spent entirely in praying, and doing penance. Whenever people say that such lives are useless and lazy, I will remember, on the contrary, that our Lord Himself has said, that certain devils can only be overcome by prayer and fasting. What better motive could there be, than Jesus Christ's own commendation, for respecting and cherishing the contemplative orders?

*Resolution.* I will remember, whenever I wish to obtain a special grace, such as a cure or a conversion, that the prayers of religious communities are very powerful in God's sight. I will then recommend my intentions to them. God blesses this confidence in the prayers of the communion of saints.

*Prayer.* I beg of Thee, O my God, to pardon the levity with which I have too frequently spoken of religious orders, and the irreverent way I have sometimes treated persons consecrated to Thee, and who obtain so many graces for an ungrateful world.

# CHAPTER LXXXIV.

## JESUS PAYETH THE DIDRACHMA.

And when they were come to Capharnaum, they that received the didrachma, came to Peter, and said to him: Doth not your master pay the didrachma?

He said: Yes. And when he was come into the house, Jesus prevented him, saying: What is thy opinion, Simon? The kings of the earth, of whom do they receive tribute or custom? of their own children, or of strangers?

And he said: Of strangers. Jesus said to him: Then the children are free.

But that we may not scandalize them, go to the sea, and cast in a hook: and that fish, which shall first come up, take: and when thou hast opened its mouth, thou shalt find a stater: take that, and give it to them for me and thee.—*St. Matthew xvii. 23-26.*

*Preparatory Prayer.* Lord, make me attentive and recollected in Thy presence, and deign to instruct me.

I. When Jesus and His disciples arrived at Capharnaum, St. Peter was asked, if His Master did not pay tribute. He replied: "Yes," and entered the house, when Jesus at once, without being questioned, spoke to St. Peter of what was troubling him. Our Lord here again gives proof of His divine power of reading our inmost thoughts. What a great consolation it would be for me, if I were thoroughly imbued with this truth, that from the tabernacle Jesus also reads in my heart, and even knows my wants before I expose them to Him. St. Peter was anxious, as he approached our Lord, to know where he should get the money, but Jesus, having explained to him that it was not necessary for the Lord of all things to pay tribute, added: "But that we may not scandalize them, go to the sea, and cast in a hook: and that fish, which shall first come up, take: and when thou hast opened its mouth, thou shalt find a stater: take that, and give it to them for Me and thee."

II. I will follow the Apostle, as he willingly and at once, with renewed confidence, obeys His Master. The prophecy is fulfilled to the letter. How great must have been St. Peter's emotion, when, on opening the fish's mouth, he found the stater or coin of four drachmas!

Our Lord preferred to work a miracle, rather than not comply with the law, although he could claim exemption from it, both as Master of the world, and Child of Israel. He here shows me, how great should be my respect for authority, and the care I should take not to give even the slightest scandal. Such is the practical lesson to be learned from this miraculous fish.

If Almighty God thus worked a miracle, so that He might Himself fulfil what seemed, so to speak, but a slight duty, I ought to understand that I should always obey promptly and willingly.

*Resolution.* I will henceforward obey at once, even when I feel great repugnance to do what I am told.

*Prayer.* O Jesus, obedient unto a miracle, and unto death, make me understand and practise the virtue of obedience.

## CHAPTER LXXXV.

### BECOME AS LITTLE CHILDREN.

At that hour the disciples came to Jesus saying: Who thinkest thou is the greater in the kingdom of heaven?

And Jesus calling unto him a little child, set him in the midst of them,

And said: Amen I say to you, unless you be converted, and become as little children, you shall not enter into the kingdom of heaven.

Whosoever therefore shall humble himself as this little child, he is the greater in the kingdom of heaven.

And he that shall receive one such little child in my name, receiveth me;

But he that shall scandalize one of these little ones that believe in me, it were better for him that a millstone should be hanged about his neck, and that he should be drowned in the depth of the sea.—*St. Matthew xviii. 1-6.*

*Preparatory Prayer.* I offer Thee, O my God, all my thoughts and aspirations during this meditation; do Thou deign to bless them.

I. Notwithstanding the lessons of humility, which Jesus had so constantly given His disciples, they had not as yet vanquished their pride, and each one, no doubt, at times compared himself favourably with his companions. Thus we see them, as they close round Jesus, anxious, in their false ideas of true glory, to hear something pleasing to their self-love, asking Him in the words of the Gospel, "Who, thinkest Thou, is the greater in the kingdom of heaven?" Does Jesus rebuke their pride, as it deserves? No! He does not even show them that such ambition is utterly opposed to all His teaching and example, but, with more than usual sweetness and kindness, He sets a little child in their midst, telling them that unless "they become as little children," they shall not enter the kingdom of heaven.

II. What a beautiful sight to see Thee thus, O Jesus, with a little child before Thee! I will try and understand the meaning of Thy words: "Whosoever therefore shall humble himself as this little child, he is the greater in the kingdom of heaven." That is to say, the more I shall lower, and think little of myself, the nearer shall I be to our Lord, and the more will He love me. Moreover, what reason have I to esteem myself?

O Mary, who wert near Jesus, at least in spirit, when He showed His disciples the little child, and told them to become like it, present me in turn to thy Divine Son, and obtain for me a true and perfect humility.

*Resolution.* I will try never to boast of any advantage, I may possess, either of family or otherwise. On the contrary, I will endeavour to bear humiliations without murmuring, or showing that I am hurt, and will even try to thank God for them.

*Prayer.* O Jesus, meek and humble of heart, bless my resolution, and enable me to keep it.

# CHAPTER LXXXVI.

## THE MAN BORN BLIND.

And Jesus passing by, seeing a man who was blind from his birth ; . . .

He spat on the ground, and made clay of the spittle, and spread the clay upon his eyes,

And said to him: Go, wash in the pool of Siloe, which is interpreted Sent. He went therefore, and washed, and he came seeing.

The neighbours therefore, and they who had seen him before that he was a beggar, said: Is not this he that sat, and begged? Some said: This is he.

But others said: No, but he is like him. But he said: I am he.

They said therefore to him: How were thy eyes opened?

He answered: That man that is called Jesus, made clay, and anointed my eyes, and said to me: Go to the pool of Siloe, and wash. And I went, I washed, and I see.

And they said to him: Where is he? He saith: I know not.

They bring him that had been blind to the Pharisees.—*St. John ix. 1: and 6-13.*

*Preparatory Prayer.* Deign, O my God, to bless this meditation, whilst I endeavour, prostrate at Thy Feet, to listen attentively to Thy word.

I. "And Jesus passing by, saw a man who was blind from his birth." Here then was one whose misfortune was well known. As a child, no doubt, his parents had hoped for his cure; but he remained blind, and those who knew him as he grew up, pitied both him and his parents, especially when he came to an age of maturity without being able to earn his living. Being thus reduced to beg, his appearance was familiar to most of his fellow townsmen. When, therefore, Jesus cured him, I can easily understand how great and general was the surprise. "Is not this he that sat and begged?" was asked of him on all sides. "Some said: This is he. But others said: No, but he is like him. But he said: I am he."

The fame of this wonderful miracle only served to increase the anger of the Pharisees; they therefore tried to deny it, and meeting him who had been blind, they attempted to puzzle and intimidate him with questions and threats.

II. The poor man, nevertheless, holds his ground. Then our Lord's enemies question his father and mother, who reply: "We know that this is our son, and that he was born blind; but how he now seeth we know not: or who hath opened his eyes we know not: ask himself; he is of age, let him speak for himself." They spoke thus, the Gospel tells us, out of fear of the Jews.

Here, then, is a subject of grave reflection for myself. How often have not I been wanting in frankness and loyalty with God, because I was afraid of being rebuked? The parents of this man feared the Jews. Am

I not afraid of my superiors, or masters, or even my brothers, sisters or companions?

At times I do not like to acknowledge a fault: at others I fear being laughed at. What petty cowardice! If I yield to fear now, how shall I, later in life, resist in grave temptations? I shall then be only too likely to commit great acts of cowardice.

*Resolution.* I will at once accustom myself to act courageously and sincerely, and will resist, with all my strength, the fear of being blamed or laughed at.

*Prayer.* Thou alone, my good Master, canst help me in carrying out this intention. Oh, do not refuse me Thy aid!

## CHAPTER LXXXVII.

### THE FAITH OF THE MAN BORN BLIND.

Jesus heard that (the Jews) had cast out (the man born blind): and when he had found him, he said to him: Dost thou believe in the Son of God?

He answered, and said: Who is he, Lord, that I may believe in him?

And Jesus said to him: Thou hast both seen him: and it is he that talketh with thee.

And he said: I believe, Lord. And falling down he adored him.—*St. John ix. 35-38.*

*Preparatory Prayer.* Direct my thoughts, O my God, so that they may be in unison with Thy holy Will.

I. After questioning the poor man a second time, the Jews dismissed him with harshness, because he persisted in giving glory to Jesus. Our Lord, hearing this, being touched no doubt with his firm resistance, contrived to meet him, so as to reward his gratitude with a yet greater grace. He had already opened his eyes to the sun's rays, now He gives him the light of faith.

How often Jesus acts thus! Unknown to all the world, He arranges and furnishes the occasion of winning souls to Himself, and then, as it were, He waits for the very moment which He has marked out.

II. When He had found him, Jesus said to him: "Dost thou believe in the Son of God?"

I will consider how happy the poor man must have been to meet Jesus again, Who had given him his sight. He looks at Him with joy and listens to Him with attention, being ready to obey Him in everything. "He answered and said: Who is He, Lord, that I may believe in Him? And Jesus said to him: Thou hast both seen Him; and it is He that talketh with thee. And he said: I believe, Lord. And falling down he adored Him."

Thus I see him prostrate at Jesus' Feet, his heart filled with joy and admiration, for he had been cured by the Son of God Himself. I fancy I behold Jesus, as He raises him with kindness, wishing to strengthen his faith and teach him all the grace of His divine presence. Let me remain a moment at our Lord's Feet, in company with this man born blind; I shall there find an admirable lesson for myself. Fidelity to grace received, and the courage of confessing God, obtained for this poor sufferer the further grace of being sought after, enlightened and instructed by Jesus Himself.

I should derive great strength from the thought that God sometimes, as I know, in reward for a slight victory won, or duty accomplished, grants an interior peace or increase of light.

Such graces must not be neglected; whenever they are vouchsafed to me, I must in spirit prostrate myself before God, and adore and thank Him, instead of yielding to external distractions and self-complacency.

*Resolution.* Whenever the grace of God shall enable me to perform an act of fidelity or courage, I will thank our Lord, knowing that, without His aid, I should never have been able to do it.

*Prayer.* Thou knowest my great weakness better than I do, my good Master. Come then to my aid, and when Thou seekest me, do not allow me to escape Thee.

## CHAPTER LXXXVIII.

### THE GOOD SHEPHERD.

I am the good shepherd : and I know mine, and mine know me.

As the Father knoweth me, and I know the Father ; and I lay down my life for my sheep.

And other sheep I have, that are not of this fold : them also I must bring, and they shall hear my voice and there shall be one fold and one shepherd.—*St. John x. 14-16.*

*Preparatory Prayer.* Be Thou, O Lord, my Shepherd and Guide. Deign to make me know Thee better, so that I may love Thee more.

I. "I am the good Shepherd." This is one of the most consoling expressions that our Saviour made use of. To understand all that is meant by it, I will call to mind what I have seen the shepherds do in the country. How anxiously they watch over their sheep, even as a mother does over her children! How lovingly they tend the lambs, and try to cure them when ill, or in pain !

When they go out to the pasturage, they keep all their sheep together, so that none may be lost, and if any danger threatens, they ward it off. Thus it is that the flock knows its shepherd, and obeys his voice.

II. When I hear our Lord say, "I am the good Shepherd: the good Shepherd giveth His life for His sheep," I should, remembering that I am one of His chosen sheep, consider what I have done, so far, to show my gratitude to my loving Saviour, Who never ceases to load me with gifts. Have I ever even thought of His numberless graces? O my God, how powerless I am to make any return for all Thy favours! I will, however, never cease to utter prayers of thanksgiving; for these, I know, are most pleasing to Thee.

Jesus adds: "And other sheep I have that are not of this fold: them also I must bring, and they shall hear My Voice, and there shall be one fold and one shepherd." This wish of Thine should teach me, O my God, with what fervour I ought to pray for the conversion of such souls as know Thee not, so that they, too, may be loved, guided and cared for by Thee. I know that Thou art pleased, when we ask for that which Thou art only longing to grant.

*Resolution.* I will set aside one day, every week, on which to offer up my prayers and actions for the conversion of sinners, and especially for those for whom I am more particularly bound to pray.

*Prayer.* Divine Shepherd of our souls, deign to cure my fickleness, so that I may be ever faithful to this resolution.

## CHAPTER LXXXIX.

### MARY AND MARTHA.

Now it came to pass as they went, that he entered into a certain town : and a certain woman named Martha, received him into her house.

And she had a sister called Mary, who sitting also at the Lord's feet, heard his word.

But Martha was busy about much serving : who stood and said : Lord, hast thou no care that my sister hath left me alone to serve? speak to her therefore, that she help me.

And the Lord answering, said to her : Martha, Martha, thou art careful, and art troubled about many things.

But one thing is necessary. Mary hath chosen the best part, which shall not be taken away from her.—*St. Luke x. 38-42.*

*Preparatory Prayer.* Help me, O my God, and deign to instruct and enlighten me.

I. The Holy Gospel frequently presents to my mind the picture of Jesus journeying through Galilee ; and this it does, in order to make me better realise His goodness, in seeking out the sick, the infirm and the ignorant, and to make me understand His divine influence over the hearts of men. Jesus passes in the midst of us also ; He blesses and instructs us, and wishes to reside within us. If my heart were only open to Him, He would enter at once and bring thousands of graces with

Him. Come, my God, into my soul, and deign always to remain there.

II. I will learn from the Gospel what I ought to do, so as to induce Jesus to come and abide with me. "A certain woman, named Martha, received Him into her house. And she had a sister called Mary who sitting also at the Lord's Feet, heard His word." What a contrast between the two sisters. Martha busies herself about all the needful preparations, so as to receive our Lord properly, while Mary remains at His Feet, silent and all absorbed in Him. I shall see directly how pleasing to Jesus was this attitude of Mary Magdalen, for, when Martha, in her anxiety, wished Him to tell her sister to come to her aid, Jesus replied: "Mary has chosen the best part which shall not be taken away from her." I should then imitate Mary, and, like her, listen attentively when Jesus speaks to me, as He does, at times, in my prayers or after Holy Communion, or when He, by suggesting good thoughts or resolutions, deigns to instruct me. I will not be satisfied with receiving Him like Martha, but will, like Mary, be attentive to His every word.

When my proneness to distraction renders this difficult, I will throw myself by her side at His Sacred Feet.

*Resolution.* To overcome my distractions, I will frequently examine myself when I pray, as to whether I, like Mary Magdalen, am really present at our Saviour's Feet.

*Prayer.* I beg of thee, great saint and faithful friend of Jesus, to offer Him my petition; obtain for me, I entreat, the grace to listen to His divine words with attention such as thine.

## CHAPTER XC.

### THE RICH MAN.

There was a certain rich man, who was clothed in purple and fine linen : and feasted sumptuously every day.

And there was a certain beggar named Lazarus, who lay at his gate, full of sores,

Desiring to be filled with the crumbs, that fell from the rich man's table, and no man did give him : moreover the dogs came and licked his sores.

And it came to pass that the beggar died, and was carried by the angels into Abraham's bosom. And the rich man also died : and he was buried in hell.

And lifting up his eyes, when he was in torments, he saw Abraham afar off, and Lazarus in his bosom :

And he cried and said : Father Abraham, have mercy on me, and send Lazarus that he may dip the tip of his finger in water, to cool my tongue, for I am tormented in this flame.

And Abraham said to him : Son, remember that thou didst receive good things in thy life-time, and likewise Lazarus evil things : but now he is comforted, and thou art tormented ;

And besides all this, between us and you there is fixed a great chaos : so that they who would pass from hence to you, cannot, nor from thence come hither.—*St. Luke xvi. 19-26.*

*Preparatory Prayer.* My God, make my mind attentive, and my heart obedient, so that I may profit by Thy holy inspirations during this meditation.

I. In to-day's meditation, Almighty God paints for

me so vivid a picture that I have only to gaze upon it, and listen attentively. First of all, I see a great contrast between the two men: the one is clothed in purple and fine linen; the other, the poor man Lazarus, has to lie on straw in the street; the former, hard-hearted and pitiless, in his life of ease and luxury, is surrounded by companions in pleasure; the latter, though dying of misery and hunger, is tended by none, save the dogs that come to lick his wounds. Similar contrasts are still to be seen in our own times. The rich, it is true, are not clothed in purple, but they are still surrounded by all that can render their lives easy, and by every luxury that the mind of man can devise. And though the good among them are far more numerous than before the coming of our Lord, yet there are alas! many who, absorbed in their riches, are only too like the description of Dives in the parable.

II. Jesus goes on: "And it came to pass that the beggar died, and was carried by the angels into Abraham's bosom. And the rich man also died: and he was buried in hell." It would be impossible to have a clearer enunciation of the promised reward of suffering. But, on the other hand, what a terrible picture of the chastisements in store for the rich selfish miser, who, after having during life wilfully abandoned himself to every pleasure, is finally condemned by divine justice to be punished for ever in hell!

Further on in the parable I see that the beggar Lazarus is given a place, after death, in Abraham's bosom, that is to say, among the elect. Our Lord mentions him by name as though to perpetuate his memory from generation to generation, and for 1800 years Lazarus' poverty in this life and his reward in the next have been familiar to all. But our Lord does not tell us the rich man's name, and all we know of him is his hardness of heart and his fall into hell. What a lesson for me, and what an inducement to be charitable!

*Resolution.* I will seriously examine my conscience and see what little luxuries I can dispense with, so as to please God, and give, with my parents' permission, as much of my pocket money as I can, to the poor.

*Prayer.* I beg of Thee, my good Master, inspire me with true sentiments of Christian and devoted charity. Teach me to love the poor, who, as Thou Thyself hast told me, will always exist in the Church.

# CHAPTER XCI.

## THE PHARISEES AND SCRIBES MURMUR AGAINST JESUS.

Now the publicans and sinners drew near unto him to hear him.

And the Pharisees and the Scribes murmured, saying: This man receiveth sinners, and eateth with them.

And he spoke to them this parable, saying:

What man of you that hath an hundred sheep: and if he shall lose one of them, doth he not leave the ninety nine in the desert, and go after that which was lost until he find it?

And when he hath found it, lay it upon his shoulders rejoicing:

And coming home call together his friends and neighbours, saying to them: Rejoice with me, because I have found my sheep that was lost?

I say to you, that even so there shall be joy in heaven upon one sinner that doth penance, more than upon ninety nine just who need not penance.—*St. Luke xv. 1-7.*

*Preparatory Prayer.* O my God, I desire that all my thoughts may be entirely consecrated to Thee during this meditation.

I. Jesus is surrounded by a crowd of publicans, for His goodness and gentle manner inspire confidence in these outcasts. They know their own wickedness, and yet have not sufficient strength to abandon their evil life. Our Lord receives them with forbearance; they, therefore, with increased confidence, frequently try to meet Him and learn from Him greater courage and strength of mind. Thus it is, that I see them pressing around Jesus, anxious to listen to His teaching, and eagerly treasuring up all that He says. Never as yet had they met with such kindness. His gentle but firm way of preaching at once spoke to their poor hardened hearts, accustomed, as they had been, to be repulsed, or treated with indifference or severity. But the Pharisees and the Scribes murmured saying: "This man receiveth sinners, and eateth with them."

II. Jesus, instead of reproaching them, propounds this simple parable: "What man of you, that hath an hundred sheep: and if he shall lose one of them, doth he not leave the ninety nine in the desert, and go after that which was lost until he find it? And when he hath found it, lay it upon his shoulders rejoicing: and coming home call together his friends, and neighbours, saying to them: Rejoice with me for I have found my sheep that was lost?"

With what forbearing charity Thou dost here, O my good Master, show the Pharisees the injustice of which they are guilty! Yet they, instead of being confounded, refuse, in their earthly wisdom, to understand Thy gentle and fatherly rebuke. I, however, O my God, will try and learn the lesson it teaches. Thy words do not only apply to the Pharisees: they condemn all feelings of envy. How often, at my age even, in my studies or play, am I not tempted to give way to love of self or jealousy? Have I not often felt inclined to encourage these great faults, especially when I have seen others more loved or praised than myself?

*Resolution.* Whenever I feel the slightest temptation to envy or jealousy, I will at once repress it, and try to nourish the opposite feelings of sympathy and interest.

*Prayer.* Thou alone, O my God, canst sustain me by Thy grace. Help me, I beg of Thee, to keep this resolution.

# CHAPTER XCII.

## LORD, TEACH US TO PRAY.

And he said to them: Which of you shall have a friend, and shall go to him at midnight, and shall say to him: Friend, lend me three loaves,

Because a friend of mine is come off his journey to me, and I have not what to set before him:

And he from within should answer and say: Trouble me not, the door is now shut, and my children are with me in bed, I cannot rise and give thee.

Yet if he shall continue knocking, I say to you, although he will not rise and give him, because he is his friend, yet because of his importunity he will rise, and give him as many as he needeth.

And I say to you, Ask: and it shall be given you: seek, and you shall find: knock and it shall be opened to you.

For every one that asketh, receiveth: and he that seeketh, findeth: and to him that knocketh, it shall be opened.

And which of you if he ask his father bread, will he give him a stone? or a fish: will he for a fish give him a serpent?

Or if he shall ask an egg: will he reach him a scorpion?

If you then being evil, know how to give good gifts to your children: how much more will your Father from heaven give the good Spirit to them that ask him?—*St. Luke xi. 5-13.*

*Preparatory Prayer.* O my God, Thou, who didst teach Thy disciples how to pray, deign, I beseech Thee, to show me how to meditate.

I. The meaning of our Lord's discourse to His disciples, as related in the eleventh chapter of St. Luke, is so clear as to need no explanation. I can easily picture to myself the man who, denied at first, continues to knock at his neighbour's door, till he obtains his request out of sheer importunity. Then Jesus adds: "Ask: and it shall be given you: seek, and you shall find: knock and it shall be opened to you. . . . And which of you, if he ask his father bread, will he give him a stone? . . . If you then being evil, know how to give good gifts to your children: how much more will your Father from heaven give the good Spirit to them that ask Him?"

Two things strike me in these words of our Lord, and cover me with confusion. First of all, Jesus' goodness. With what patience and solicitude He explains His meaning to us all. I can never weary of considering how our Divine Lord, in order to fix His disciples attention, seeks out the most familiar comparisons.

II. Then, too, with what care does not Jesus try to enkindle in us a filial confidence in God? Instead of saying, "My Father," as was His wont, He here says, "Your Father from Heaven," just as to a child, when it desires to obtain something from its parents, one says, by way of encouragement, "Go and ask your father or mother, they are so good and kind." So when I pray to God in Heaven I should do it with confidence, being fully persuaded that, if I ask Him for bread, He will not give me a stone. I should learn from these comparisons to enter into the smallest details in my prayers. I should ask, not merely for great graces, such as blessings for the Church and my family, or even the necessary virtues for myself, but also some particular little victory over self, success in my studies, patience and mildness of temper in my small trials, and every little thing I need in my daily life.

*Resolution.* I will try to cultivate a spirit of prayer, by to-day continually asking of God the grace necessary for each circumstance as it arises.

*Prayer.* Instil into me, O my good Master, the spirit of confident prayer, such as Thou art pleased to find in the hearts and on the lips of Thy children.

# CHAPTER XCIII.

## ZACCHEUS.

And entering in, he walked through Jericho.

And behold there was a man named Zaccheus: who was the chief of the publicans, and he was rich:

And he sought to see Jesus who he was: and he could not for the crowd, because he was low of stature.

And running before, he climbed up into a sycamore tree that he might see him: for he was to pass that way.

And when Jesus was come to the place, looking up, he saw him, and said to him: Zaccheus make haste and come down: for this day I must abide in thy house.

And he made haste and came down, and received him with joy.

And when all saw it, they murmured, saying that he was gone to be a guest with a man that was a sinner.

But Zaccheus standing said to the Lord: Behold, Lord, the half of my goods I give to the poor: and if I have wronged any man of anything, I restore him four-fold.

Jesus said to him: This day is salvation come to this house: because he also is a son of Abraham.

For the Son of man is come to seek and to save that which was lost. —*St. Luke xix. 1-10.*

*Preparatory Prayer.* Deign, O God, to give me an earnest desire of knowing and loving Thee more and more.

I. St. Luke tells us that, when Jesus was travelling through Jericho, Zaccheus was anxious to see and know Him. He had heard of our Lord, and probably the account of His actions, had already by the workings of an interior grace, aroused in him a first good desire, viz., that of seeing our Saviour. The crowd, however, was great round Jesus, and as Zaccheus was small of stature, he had to run on in front and climb up a tree, in order to see better. He was a publican, even the chief of the publicans at Jericho. These men, though originally they had merely to collect the revenue, had become so notorious for their dishonest dealings and worse, that, in the time of our Lord, they were utterly despised and contemned. And yet this poor sinner is docile to the first inspiration of grace, and, in his eagerness to see Jesus, he watches, from his hiding-place in the tree, the passing of our Lord, gazing earnestly on Him, and on Him alone.

II. "Jesus, looking up, saw him, and said to him: Zaccheus, make haste and come down: for this day I must abide in thy house. And he made haste and came down, and received Him with joy." And with a thoroughness, that should serve as a model for a true conversion, said to the Lord: "Behold, Lord, the half of my goods I give to the poor: and if I have wronged any man of any thing, I restore him four-fold."

What a happy result of his eagerness to see Jesus! I should here learn a practical lesson. Whither shall I go to seek our Lord? Must I, like Zaccheus, be at great pains to outstrip the crowd, so as to be able to see Him pass? Ah, no! My Saviour is always near me, and day and night, patiently waits for me in the tabernacle, ready to fill my heart with His most abundant graces. As He saw Zaccheus, He sees me too. Whenever I go to church, into the presence of the Blessed Sacrament, how many graces God grants me for myself, my friends, and those for whom I pray, and these graces are like those accorded by Jesus to Zaccheus for himself, his house and family.

*Resolution.* Whenever I can, I will spend at least a few minutes every day, before the Blessed Sacrament, and will try to be very recollected in the presence of Jesus.

*Prayer.* I beg of Thee, beforehand, O my God, to grant me Thy choicest graces, whenever I am in Thy holy presence.

## CHAPTER XCIV.

### THE ILLNESS OF LAZARUS.

Now there was a certain man sick named Lazarus, of Bethania, of the town of Mary and of Martha her sister.

(And Mary was she that anointed the Lord with ointment and wiped his feet with her hair: whose brother Lazarus was sick.)

His sisters therefore sent to him, saying: Lord, behold, he whom thou lovest, is sick.—*St. John xi. 1-3.*

*Preparatory Prayer.* O Jesus, make me meditate with attention, so that I may know and follow Thee faithfully.

I. Before studying the wonderful miracle of the raising of Lazarus to life, I wish to make myself thoroughly acquainted with his family, who were so loved by our Lord. The Gospel tells me that Lazarus, Martha and Mary lived at Bethania. I have seen Mary, a penitent in the house of Simon the Pharisee, washing with her tears the Feet of Jesus, and listening to Him with the deepest attention. I remember too, how great was Martha's eagerness to receive our Lord into her house. And I know that whenever He was at Jerusalem, which is not far from Bethania, He frequently used to go there, to rest from the fatigues of His preaching. Thus it is, that this chosen family is so well known, even down to the present time, and the name of their town so closely associated with the enjoyment of their privileged intimacy and union with the very Heart of our dear Lord.

II. While Jesus is away, Lazarus falls ill. Oh, how Martha and Mary regret His absence, Who has cured so many sick people; for they know that Lazarus has, as it were, more right than others to expect such a favour at the hands of his Divine Master and Friend. In their affliction and grief, they make common cause of sorrow. The disease, however, becomes worse, and their anxiety is redoubled. They are in doubt as to whether they ought not to send for Jesus and ask Him to interrupt His Apostolic labours, so that He may come to their sick brother. At length, the danger having increased, they hesitate no longer, but send a messenger to Jesus, saying: "Lord, behold, he whom Thou lovest, is sick." What a simple prayer their message contains, and yet how full it is of faith and confidence! It should be a model for me, in anxiety and trouble. Although Almighty God knows perfectly well the cause of my grief, still He wishes me to lay my trouble before Him; and then I must patiently wait, until, in His mercy, He deigns to afford me relief.

*Resolution.* I will always ask God for whatever I wish to obtain, without yielding to discouragement or anxiety, and I will ever try to strengthen and increase my filial confidence in Him.

*Prayer.* Instil into my heart, O Lord, feelings of love and confidence, so that I may resemble Thy holy friends at Bethania.

# CHAPTER XCV.

## THE ILLNESS OF LAZARUS.—JESUS' RETURN.

These things he said, and after that he said to them: Lazarus our friend sleepeth: but I go that I may awake him out of sleep.

His disciples therefore said: Lord, if he sleep, he shall do well.

But Jesus spoke of his death and they thought that he spoke of the repose of sleep,

Then therefore Jesus said to them plainly. Lazarus is dead:
. . . . . . . . .
Jesus therefore came: and found that he had been four days already in the grave.
. . . . . . . . .
Martha therefore, as soon as she heard that Jesus was come, went to meet him: but Mary sat at home.

Martha therefore said to Jesus: Lord, if thou hadst been here, my brother had not died:

But now also I know that whatsoever thou wilt ask of God, God will give it thee.

Jesus saith to her: Thy brother shall rise again.—*St. John xi. 11-14, 17, and 20-23.*

*Preparatory Prayer.* Behold me at Thy Feet, O Jesus, speak to my heart of Thy love for me, and increase, I beseech Thee, its love for Thee.

I. I will meditate on these words of our Lord, "Lazarus our friend sleepeth: but I go that I may awake him out of sleep." Jesus knew that His disciples would not at once understand His meaning, when He said, "Lazarus sleepeth:" and that He would have to tell them openly, a little later, that he was dead. Why then did He say "Lazarus sleepeth?" Probably to make us understand that death is, in reality, but a rest or slumber, from which, one day, we shall be awakened to the true life of eternity. And, in speaking thus, Jesus did not think of His disciples alone. He knew that the Church would adopt this expression of His, and would always speak of death as the Christian's sleep, and that, through all ages, she would pray for the dead asleep in Christ, asking Him to grant them eternal rest. This thought became so familiar to the early Christians, that at every step in the catacombs at Rome, one meets with sepulchral inscriptions announcing that such a one is asleep, and awaiting the call to eternal life.

Though I am young, yet do I not already miss many familiar faces, that once I knew? The idea of death is so terrible to nature, that these consoling words of our Lord go to my very heart. I will pause, then, a moment, and thank Thee, O my God, for teaching me that death is but a slumber, and that, like Lazarus, we shall live again, and for ever, in heaven.

II. Jesus once more turns His steps towards Bethania. He knows how bitterly the sisters of Lazarus mourn his loss, and His pity is all the greater, when Martha hurries out to meet Him, saying humbly: "Lord, if Thou hadst been here my brother had not died. But now also I know that whatsoever Thou wilt ask of God, God will give it Thee." He is therefore at once moved by this act of faith, and replies: "Thy brother shall rise again," adding: "I am the Resurrection and the Life."

Martha remains fondly clinging to Thy words, O Lord, for though she has heard Thy blessed assurance, she is afraid that Thou art only speaking of the future resurrection, and she saith: "I know that he shall rise again in the resurrection at the last day."

Jesus requires a more explicit act of faith, and questions her, so as to make her reply: "Yea, Lord, I have believed that Thou art Christ, the Son of the living God, Who art come into this world."

Teach me again, O Jesus, as Thou hast often taught me in the Gospel, the efficacy of an act of faith.

*Resolution.* I will frequently enkindle my confidence by such acts, and often beg for a lively faith, and regard it as the greatest of treasures.

*Prayer.* Deign, O Lord, to increase my faith, and to render it firm, lively and strong, alike in sorrow as in joy.

# CHAPTER XCVI.

## THE RAISING OF LAZARUS TO LIFE.

And Jesus wept.

The Jews therefore said: Behold how he loved him.

But some of them said: Could not he that opened the eyes of the man born blind, have caused that this man should not die?

Jesus therefore again groaning in himself, cometh to the sepulchre; now it was a cave: and a stone was laid over it.

Jesus saith: Take away the stone. Martha the sister of him that was dead, saith to him: Lord, by this time he stinketh, for he is now of four days.

Jesus saith to her: Did not I say to thee, that if thou wilt believe, thou shalt see the glory of God?

They took therefore the stone away: and Jesus lifting up his eyes, said: Father, I give thee thanks that thou hast heard me.

And I knew that thou hearest me always, but because of the people who stand about have I said it; that they may believe that thou hast sent me.

When he had said these things, he cried with a loud voice: Lazarus, come forth.

And presently he that had been dead came forth.—*St. John xi. 35-44.*

*Preparatory Prayer.* Show me, O Lord, how much Thou lovest us. Teach me how to love my relations, and yet refer all my affection to Thee.

I. After Martha and Mary had affirmed their faith, our Lord, turning to the Jews, said: "Where have you laid him? They say to Him: Lord, come and see. And Jesus wept. The Jews therefore said: Behold how He loved him." St. John then tells us that "Jesus groaned in the spirit and troubled Himself." I will therefore contemplate my God overcome with sorrow and weeping for His friend! What must have been the expression of His adorable Countenance, and of His whole Person in His struggle with nature? Though He never lost His self-possession, yet Jesus suffered, and permitted His tears to flow, so as to show us that we are allowed this comfort in our troubles. But our Lord is more affected by the woe of others, than by His own, and in His love and pity, He hastens to reach the tomb. "Jesus therefore again groaning in Himself cometh to the sepulchre: now it was a cave; and a stone was laid over it. Jesus saith: Take away the stone." The Jews obeyed: and thus I see death brought face to face with the Author of life.

II. Jesus, having again consoled Martha, raised His eyes to heaven, and invoking His Father, "cried with a loud voice: Lazarus, come forth." What a scene is here! The bereft relations, the friends that had come to console them, and the crowd that followed Jesus, are all pressing around the sepulchre. They wait, listen and watch. Then, as the Holy Gospel tells us, "presently he that had been dead came forth bound feet and hands with winding bands, and his face was bound about with a napkin. Jesus said to them: Loose him and let him go."

The bystanders at once obey our Lord, and free Lazarus from the bands, with which, according to the Jewish custom of burial, he had been bound. His first act is certainly to adore and thank his Lord, while Martha and Mary, in their transports of joy, are loud in their thanksgiving.

I bless Thee, O my God, for this new miracle, and I beg of Thee to teach me the lessons I should learn from it. Ought I not to understand from seeing Thee thus console and encourage the sisters of Lazarus, and restore their faith, that in family troubles I should forget myself, and think of the affliction of those around me?

*Resolution.* When my parents have any grief or anxiety, I will overcome my own sorrow, and console them by my devoted and loving sympathy.

*Prayer.* Teach me, O my God, how to forget myself completely and think only of others.

# CHAPTER XCVII.

## THE DISCIPLES PREPARE THE PASCH.

And the day of the unleavened bread came, on which it was necessary that the Pasch should be killed.

And he sent Peter and John, saying: Go and prepare for us the Pasch, that we may eat.

But they said: Where wilt thou that we prepare?

And he said to them: Behold, as you go into the city, there shall meet you a man carrying a pitcher of water: follow him into the house where he entereth in.

And you shall say to the good man of the house: The master saith to thee: Where is the guest-chamber, where I may eat the Pasch with my disciples?

And he will show you a large dining-room furnished, and there prepare.

And they going, found as he had said to them, and made ready the Pasch.—*St. Luke xxii. 7-13.*

*Preparatory Prayer.* Thy last hour, O Lord, is now approaching, when Thou art to sacrifice Thyself for me: make me, then, more and more attentive.

I. All Jewish families were bound by the laws to eat the Pasch on the days called the Azymes. The Evangelist, then, brings us to those days: but where is our Lord to assemble His chosen disciples, since, in His life of poverty, He has no home? Still, though Jesus never works a miracle for His own relief, He will not allow His destitute state to be the cause of any infringement of the law; therefore, sending Peter and John, He said to them: "Behold, as you go into the city, there shall meet you a man carrying a pitcher of water: follow him where he entereth in. And you shall say to the good man of the house: The Master saith to thee: Where is the guest-chamber, where I may eat the Pasch with My disciples? And he will show you a large dining-room furnished, and there prepare. And they going, found as He had said to them, and made ready the Pasch." I have often read this passage of the Holy Gospel, without noticing how exactly Jesus' prediction was fulfilled to the letter. What confidence this should give me in our Lord, Who has also told us that not a single hair shall fall from our heads except by His express Will. God has not only created me and given me the means of existence, but He keeps dangers far from me, and at every moment of my life knows where I am and what I am doing. He directs my steps, and even on my account does He command the angels, creatures and the elements, and regulate the course of events according to my needs of soul and body.

II. What return can I make for such care on the part of my All-powerful God? St. Luke teaches me what I ought to do. I must have a large room ready to receive Him; for this it is that the Lord requires to celebrate the Pasch. Whenever, then, I receive Jesus in Holy Communion, my heart should be carefully prepared for His coming, as was the dining-room for our Lord's Pasch at Jerusalem. This preparation should be remote, as well as immediate. Immediate in recollectedness; remote in continually endeavouring, by the constant practice of sound virtue, to overcome myself and the dominant passion which is pointed out to me, by my parents or confessor, as the bar to my advancing in piety.

*Resolution.* I will fix my attention, so easily distracted, by multiplying my acts of love, confidence and sacrifice, before receiving our Lord; and after Holy Communion I will listen to the voice of Jesus in my heart and will obey Him faithfully.

*Prayer.* Thou often givest Thyself to me, O Lord, in Holy Communion; grant that each time I have the happiness of receiving Thee, I may become less unworthy of so great a grace.

## CHAPTER XCVIII.

### CHRIST WASHETH HIS DISCIPLES' FEET.

He riseth from supper, and layeth aside his garments : and having taken a towel, girded himself.

After that, he putteth water into a basin, and began to wash the feet of the disciples, and to wipe them with the towel, wherewith he was girded.

He cometh therefore to Simon Peter. And Peter saith to him : Lord, dost thou wash my feet ?

Jesus answered, and said to him : What I do, thou knowest not now, but thou shalt know hereafter.

Peter saith to him : Thou shalt never wash my feet. Jesus answered him : If I wash thee not, thou shalt have no part with me.

Simon Peter saith to him : Lord, not only my feet, but also my hands and my head.—*St. John xiii. 4-9.*

*Preparatory Prayer.* Bless my good intention, O Lord, and deign to teach me what I should do, in order to please Thee.

I. The disciples are supping with Jesus, but, despite their sweet familiar intercourse with our Lord, I notice a shade of sorrow on their faces, for He is now speaking openly of His approaching separation from them. He foretells His death clearly, without using any more parables to refer to it. When the repast is done, Jesus rises, and, like a common servant, goes up to each of His disciples and washes his feet. In the East, in our Lord's time, this was frequently done as a special mark of honour. Thus the disciples are surprised to see Jesus do it for them. They look inquiringly from one to another, while their Master, in His sweet humble way, calmly performs this task for each of them without exception.

II. St. Peter, however, saith to Him: "Lord, dost Thou wash my feet?" and declares that he will not allow it. I can understand the warmth with which the Apostle refuses to permit his God to stoop before him, and perform this menial office. But Jesus insists, and explains that, if he wishes to share in the graces to come, he must first obey without resistance. St. Peter, therefore, making an effort to overcome himself, allows our Lord to proceed. From this meditation on Jesus' humility in washing the Apostles' feet, I should learn two distinct lessons. First of all, profiting by His example, and forgetful of self, I will always consider myself the least of all, and never think that I ought to be treated with deference. If my parents' position is such as to enable me to be served, I will always be kind and indulgent to those who wait upon me, never losing an opportunity of thanking them and showing an interest in their welfare. Secondly, Jesus chose the moment immediately before the institution of the Blessed Eucharist, to wash His Apostles' feet, in order to show me how pure my heart should be to receive Him. O Lord, make me realise this, and help me ever to purify my conscience, by perfect contrition and a sincere confession, before each of my Communions.

*Resolution.* Never to let my confessions become a matter of habit, but to pray earnestly each time, exciting my contrition and begging of God to supply what is wanting.

*Prayer.* Grant me the grace, O my dear Lord, to understand the importance of a good preparation for Confession and Communion.

## CHAPTER XCIX.

### THE LAST SUPPER.

And taking bread, he gave thanks, and brake: and gave to them, saying: This is my body which is given for you: do this for a commemoration of me.

In like manner the chalice also, after he had supped, saying: This is the chalice, the new testament in my blood, which shall be shed for you.—*St. Luke xxii. 19, 20.*

*Preparatory Prayer.* Make me more than ever attentive, O Lord Jesus, and fill my heart with Thy divine spirit.

I. After having humbly washed His Apostles' feet, Jesus returns to table with them. And here I should be most attentive, for the smallest details are important. The disciples are silent, and deeply impressed by what is taking place: Jesus' kindness and affection have overcome them. Let me see in what order they are seated. St. John, called in the Gospel the disciple whom Jesus loved, though the youngest amongst them, is close to our Lord, and indeed he merited this place of honour. None was so faithfully attached to Jesus as he, and, as I shall see, he never again leaves his Master, not even after His Crucifixion and Death, until he has buried and laid Him in the tomb.

O loved disciple of our Lord, obtain for me an increase

of attention at this solemn moment, remembering that thou wert privileged to lay thy head on Jesus' Bosom, and there make thy first thanksgiving after Communion. Ask our Lord to fill my heart with love and gratitude.

II. Everything in the Gospel history of what is about to follow is so grand, that I dare not trust myself to examine the words, but will borrow some reflections from St. Bonaventure.

" We cannot but behold with astonishment the most beloved condescension and sublime charity, with which Jesus vouchsafed to give Himself to us, ordaining the Sacrament of the Blessed Eucharist as a means whereby He might leave us that divine and heavenly Food of His sacred Body and Blood. Wherefore after He had washed His disciples' feet, to show them the ending of the sacrifices of the Old Law, and the beginning of the New Testament, and to make Himself our own true Sacrifice, He took bread into His blessed Hand, and lifting up His Eyes to His Heavenly Father, He blessed it and instituted the Sacrament of His Body, and giving It to His disciples, said: *Take, and eat, for this is My Body, Which is given for you.* And in the same manner He took the chalice and said: *Drink ye all of this. For this is My Blood of the New Testament, Which shall be shed for many unto remission of sins.* Here attentively consider how devoutly, how diligently, and how truly our Blessed Lord Jesus changed the substance of the bread into His precious Body, and afterwards with His own blessed Hands distributed Himself to that beloved and holy company, enjoining them to keep It as a memorial of His love, saying: *Do this in remembrance of Me.*"

Then the Holy Gospel gives us what is called, "The discourse after the last supper." It is the most touching bequest of a loving father to his children. How I love to contemplate the kind and thoughtful expression which Jesus' Face now wears. It is both sublime and grave. St. John, too, attracts my attention, as his head gently reclines on His loved Master's Bosom. What union exists between their two souls!

*Resolution.* I will ask St. John, when I communicate, to obtain for me a close union with our Lord.

*Prayer.* O Jesus, teach me to love Thee as dearly as did Thy chosen disciple.

## CHAPTER C.

### GETHSEMANI.

And going out he went according to his custom to the Mount of Olives. And his disciples also followed him.

And when he was come to the place, he said to them: Pray, lest ye enter into temptation.

And he was withdrawn away from them a stone's cast: and kneeling down he prayed,

Saying: Father, if thou wilt, remove this chalice from me: But yet not my will, but thine be done.

And there appeared to him an Angel from heaven, strengthening him. And being in an agony, he prayed the longer.

And his sweat became as drops of blood trickling down upon the ground.

And when he rose up from prayer, and was come to his disciples, he found them sleeping for sorrow.

And he said to them: Why sleep you? arise, pray, lest you enter into temptation. —*St. Luke xxii. 39-46.*

*Preparatory Prayer.* Deign to enter my heart, O my God, and inspire it with compassion and love.

I. The supper being finished, Jesus rises and, followed by His disciples, turns His steps towards the Garden of Olives, called Gethsemani, where He was wont to pray. On this occasion all is sad and solemn. Our Lord knows that His hour has come, and He is aware that Judas, who sold Him, the evening before, for thirty pieces of silver, is even now seeking the cohort that are to arrest his Master. The disciples, however, do not know the precise moment of the danger, but they are still impressed by all that has just taken place, the washing of their feet, Jesus' adorable discourse and loving bequest. They feel that the dreaded separation is approaching, and, seized with fear, and overcome by sorrow, they follow our Lord in silence.

II. I fancy I perceive this little chosen band going along in the dark. The gloom of night adds to their apprehension of some terrible event close at hand. Then Jesus takes SS. Peter, James and John with Him, leaving the other disciples at the gate of the garden. He wishes to proceed further Himself, to a perfectly solitary place, where a bare cavern in the rock is to witness His agony. Agony, that is the dreadful moment that precedes death; every one must pass through it, though some suffer more and longer than others. At such a time, dying people are generally surrounded by their relations or devoted friends; but Jesus has no one: He is absolutely alone, His very disciples having gone to sleep! He is suffering a terrible agony. As God, He knows everything that is about to happen, His Passion, His abandonment by His disciples, His Crucifixion, the sins of all the world, for which He is offering Himself up to the Divine Justice, and worst of all, the boundless ingratitude of men. His human nature yields to His sufferings, and I behold Him prostrate on the ground before His Father and His Judge, bathed in a sweat of blood. O my God, make me feel what Thou art suffering, make me share Thy grief! Let me bear Thee company, though I am so powerless, so miserable, for see, my heart is broken with Thine! I offer Thee beforehand all the anxieties, griefs and sufferings of my whole life; deign to accept them, O Lord. Ah! would that this poor offering of mine could afford Thee any consolation in Thy agony!

*Resolution.* To make some little sacrifice, every Friday, in union with my Saviour's Passion.

*Prayer.* O Jesus, teach me the meaning of all Thy sufferings in the garden of Olives, and make me love and console Thee for them.

## CHAPTER CI.

### THE TRAITOR'S KISS.

Then he cometh to his disciples, and saith to them: Sleep ye now and take your rest: behold the hour is at hand, and the Son of man shall be betrayed into the hands of sinners.

Rise, let us go: behold he is at hand that will betray me.

As he yet spoke, behold Judas one of the twelve came, and with him a great multitude with swords and clubs, sent from the chief priests and the ancients of the people.

And he that betrayed him, gave them a sign, saying: Whomsoever I shall kiss, that is he, hold him fast.

And forthwith coming to Jesus, he said: Hail Rabbi. And he kissed him.

And Jesus said to him: Friend, whereto art thou come? Then they came up, and laid hands on Jesus, and held him.— *St. Matthew xxvi. 45-50.*

*Preparatory Prayer.* Make me, O my God, more and more sorrowful and penitent, as I proceed further with the contemplation of Thy Passion.

I. Jesus, when in His great agony, after having prayed and freely accepted His Father's Will, was comforted by an angel from heaven. He then returned to His disciples, and said: "Rise, let us go: behold he is at hand that will betray Me." Almost before He had finished speaking, an armed band appeared, with Judas at its head, who at once advanced and kissed our Lord, thereby betraying Him. Oh, what a scene! Jesus, Who, in His Omnipotence, could at once annihilate Judas, yet submits to be kissed by him, and then allows Himself to be apprehended like a common thief. The traitor and hypocrite calls Him Master, as he salutes Him and signals Him out to the band of ruffians, who are about to lead Him to death. The disciples, alas! thunderstruck and terrified, abandon Jesus, and thus is fulfilled the prophecy which He spoke to them but a few hours before: "I will strike the Shepherd, and the flock shall be dispersed."

II. And I, what shall I do at this terrible moment? I will follow Jesus, or rather accompany Him in His rapid course, by considering with St. Bonaventure, "How those vile wretches led Him from the river Cedron, where they apprehended Him, towards the city of Jerusalem, with great haste, pain and violence—with His blessed Hands bound behind Him, as if He had been some grievous malefactor, and His garment torn from Him,—bare-headed, and stooping through the great haste and violent pain."

Alas! the savage band that hurries Thee along, O my God, is often to be found near me, quite close to me, and even within me; for whenever I listen to the promptings of anger, pride, vanity or laziness, I give myself over to my passions, and lose my freedom of action. O my good Master, I beg of Thee, impress this truth upon me now in such a manner, that later, when my passions become stronger, temptations more dangerous, and the struggle fiercer, I may remember how these demons of men hurried Thee along!

May I, at such moments, never forget how my Saviour endured all these outrages like an innocent Lamb, in order to preserve me from danger; how He allowed Himself to be bound Hand and Foot, to leave me free, and gain for me strength in temptation; and how He suffered death to save my soul.

*Resolution.* I will often pray to Jesus to deliver me from temptation.

*Prayer.* I beseech Thee, O my Divine Saviour, make me understand the strength I ought to draw from the remembrance of Thy Passion.

## CHAPTER CII.

### THE BLESSED VIRGIN AND ST. JOHN.

But they cried out: Away with him, away with him, crucify him. Pilate saith to them: Shall I crucify your king? The chief priests answered: We have no king but Cæsar.
Then therefore he delivered him to them to be crucified. And they took Jesus, and led him forth.
And bearing his own cross he went forth to that place which is called Calvary, but in Hebrew Golgotha. —*St. John xix. 15-17.*
And there followed him a great multitude of people, and of women: who bewailed and lamented him.—*St. Luke xxiii. 27.*

*Preparatory Prayer.* Deign, O Lord, to make me fully understand this meditation.

I. I have already seen Jesus seized by His enemies, and hurried off to Jerusalem. In spirit I enter Herod's palace, and there behold the meek Lamb silently suffer the greatest indignities, so that my mind and heart lead me at once to think of our Blessed Lady. Where was she during Jesus' agony? Where is she now, whilst her Son submits to all the outrages His executioners heap upon Him? Most probably He had made known to her beforehand every detail of His Passion. During His agony she must have prayed in unison with Him! And now, as she pictures to herself how her Divine Son is being cruelly beaten, scourged and spit upon, the sword of sorrow, foretold by Simeon, pierces deeper into her heart. At Nazareth, Jesus had often explained to her the prophecies relating to the Son of man, and now this is the hour of their terrible accomplishment. Her cruel sufferings are intensified by the approach of St. John, whom a Doctor of the Church represents as hastening to Mary and her companions in the house of Magdalen, and relating to them what had taken place.

II. O Mary, I will remain by thy side through all this dreadful night. I am not worthy to suffer with Jesus, especially as I have, alas! only contributed by my sins to reduce Him to this piteous state. I am indeed one of His executioners. Though I dare not approach Him, yet allow me to follow thee on thy dreary way. I again behold Jesus as He staggers along under the weight of the Cross. "His blessed and afflicted Mother," as St. Bonaventure tells us, "seeing that she could not approach Him, on account of the crowd that pressed around Him, went with St. John, and the rest of her companions, a nearer way, so that she might meet Him at the turn of the street. And when she perceived Him coming, over-loaded with the heavy Tree of the Cross, which she had not seen before, she was like one beside herself, and half dead with sorrow, so that she could neither speak to Him, nor He to her on account of the furious mob, which hurried Him along with great violence and compulsion. After however that He had gone a little way, He turned back to the women that followed weeping, and *comforted them:* and (later on) He prayed for His afflicted mother, beseeching His Father to assuage and lessen her grief."

O dearest Mother, the sword that pierces thy heart, rends mine also.

*Resolution.* In my family sorrows and personal griefs, I will seek strength in the remembrance of our Lady's compassion.

*Prayer.* O Mother of sorrows, assist all those who are in grief, teach them to gain strength and courage in fleeing to thy broken heart.

## CHAPTER CIII.

### CALVARY.

And bearing his own cross he went forth to that place which is called Calvary, but in Hebrew Golgotha:

Where they crucified him, and with him two others, one on each side, and Jesus in the midst.

. . . . . . . . . .

Now there stood by the cross of Jesus, his mother, and his mother's sister, Mary of Cleophas, and Mary Magdalen.

When Jesus therefore had seen his mother and the disciple standing, whom he loved, he said to his mother: Woman, behold thy son.

After that, he saith to the disciple: Behold thy mother. And from that hour the disciple took her to his own.

Afterwards Jesus knowing that all things were now accomplished, that the Scripture might be fulfilled, said: I thirst.

Now there was a vessel set there full of vinegar. And they putting a sponge full of vinegar about hyssop, put it to his mouth.

Jesus therefore when he had taken the vinegar, said: It is consummated. And bowing his head, he gave up the ghost.—*St. John xix. 17, 18, 25-30.*

*Preparatory Prayer.* O Mary, my loved Mother, I wish to remain with thee at the Feet of Jesus Crucified.

I. Once outside the town, Mary is able to follow Jesus at a distance, as He carries His Cross to the very top of the hill called Golgotha, and there sees Him stripped of His garments, and nailed to His ignominious Cross. Each blow of the hammer strikes home to her own heart. She then sees the Cross raised aloft, and on it her Son crucified between two thieves. O Mother of Dolours, I beg of thee, penetrate me with the thought of thy terrible suffering. I see thy silent grief, thine eyes fixed on thy Son, whilst thy heart treasures up all the words that fall from His dying Lips. "Now there stood by the Cross of Jesus, His Mother, and His Mother's sister, Mary of Cleophas, and Mary Magdalen." Let me remain with Mary at the foot of Thy Cross, O Lord, and with great reverence, in company with the holy women, with Magdalen and St. John, who remained faithful to Thee to the end, be a witness of Thy cruel death. I behold Thee, O my God, Thy strength failing, enduring every mental and physical anguish, and all this for me. Yet Jesus' love for those dear to Him is stronger than all. His Heart is torn at the sight of Mary's sufferings, and at the thought of how lonely she and the disciples will be after His death.

II. "When Jesus therefore had seen His Mother and the disciple standing whom He loved, He saith to His Mother: Woman, behold thy Son. After that He saith to the disciple: Behold thy Mother." The Church teaches us that St. John here represents all the human race, and that thus our Lady is given as a Mother to each of us. I have, therefore, dearest

Mother, now more right than ever to remember that I am thy child, that I love thee dearly, and that my heart feels and shares the sufferings with which thine is torn. And so, when Jesus in His death-throes, having fulfilled every prophecy concerning Him, utters a loud cry and dies, permit me, O Mary, to come still closer to thee. The fear and terror with which this awful scene inspires me are increased by the sudden darkness that hides everything, and yet thy grief touches my heart more deeply still!

*Resolution.* I will often ask Jesus to make me very devout to the Immaculate and Afflicted Heart of Mary, so that I may never forget its sufferings, and the sword of sorrow that pierced it through and through.

*Prayer.* Immaculate Heart of Mary, obtain for me the grace of divine love.

## CHAPTER CIV.

#### JESUS' SIDE IS OPENED WITH A SPEAR.

Then the Jews (because it was the parasceve), that the bodies might not remain upon the cross on the sabbath-day (for that was a great sabbath-day), besought Pilate that their legs might be broken, and that they might be taken away.

The soldiers therefore came: and they broke the legs of the first, and of the other that was crucified with him.

But after they were come to Jesus, when they saw that he was already dead, they did not break his legs.

But one of the soldiers with a spear opened his side, and immediately there came out blood and water.—*St. John xix. 31-34.*

*Preparatory Prayer.* I will remain on Calvary with Mary, my Mother. Grant, O Jesus, that I may there gain a great increase of love.

I. Mary, St. John and the holy women are at the foot of the Cross. Though they are united in one common sorrow, I notice that their mode of expressing it is different. Mary stands near the Cross, as the Church represents her to us in the "Stabat Mater," while St. John keeps close to her, watching her respectfully. His Divine Master in giving her to him for his Mother, commanded him to take care of her, and to sink, as it were, his own grief in his devotion to

Mary. I can easily understand all that St. John is suffering, by calling to mind my sorrow, when I have seen my mother in trouble. Mary Magdalen gives free vent to her tears: her despair is so terrible that the other holy women, themselves more calm in their desolation, essay to quiet her. This scene should teach me that in moments of family suffering, when, in the midst of the greatest grief, I hear different opinions expressed around me, I ought to be very patient and charitable in bearing others' sorrow, though it be quite different from my own. I should be careful not to hurt the feelings of others by trying to make them adopt my own way of thinking. Whenever I hear persons spoken of as strange or silly, because they exhibit their grief in an unusual manner, I should remember, instead of being tempted to laugh or criticise, that sorrow is always noble and full of dignity.

II. A new and terrible trial is at hand. Mary sees soldiers approach, and surround the Cross of Jesus and those of the thieves. The latter are still alive, so the soldiers break their legs, and thus cruelly despatch them. Mary trembles for fear lest the dead Body of her dear Son should be still further outraged. "But after they were come to Jesus, when they saw that He was already dead, they did not break His Legs. But one of the soldiers with a spear opened His Side and immediately there came out Blood and Water." O Jesus, my dear Redeemer, Thou art not then content to save me by dying for me, Thou wishest further to have Thy Sacred Side pierced, so as to give me Thy adorable Heart! I will then take refuge in that Sacred Heart, and there learn to love and imitate Thee. What greater, better or more complete gift can there be than the gift of the heart? The first prayer I was taught to lisp, as a little child, and before I understood its meaning, was: 'My God, I give Thee my heart.' To-day, it is Thou Who sayest to me: My child, I give thee My Heart.

*Resolution.* I will make myself familiar with the invocation: "Sacred Heart of Jesus, I give Thee my heart."

*Prayer.* Inflame my heart, O Lord, with love for Thy adorable Heart.

## CHAPTER CV.

### THE RETURN TO JERUSALEM.

And thy own soul a sword shall pierce.—*St. Luke ii. 35*.
O all ye that pass by the way, attend and see if there be any sorrow like to my sorrow.—*Lamentations of Jeremias i. 12*.

*Preparatory Prayer.* My God, make me very recollected; inspire my heart with feelings of love and compassion.

I. I wish to remain with Mary and be present with her at the taking down from the Cross. I witness her unutterable grief, when Nicodemus, St. Joseph of Arimathea and St. John place the lifeless Body of Jesus in the arms of His Mother. She kisses It with respect, while shedding floods of tears. O Mary, forget, I beg of thee, in thy desolation, that by my sins I am one of thy Son's executioners. Do not repulse me now, who didst once at the Crib allow me to kneel before this same Jesus, when thou didst hold Him in thy arms as a little child, and cover Him with kisses. But alas, how diffcrent it is now! I see the dead Body of my dearest Jesus, not only motionless and livid in death, but torn and disfigured by all the ignominious sufferings He has endured for my sake: the Scourging at the pillar, the Crowning with thorns, and the Crucifixion. O Jesus, if I loved Thee at Bethlehem, how much more should I not love Thee on Calvary?

But Mary does not long enjoy even the sad comfort of being able to weep over her Son's Body. It becomes necessary to bury Jesus, so, once more with her, I see Him borne away to the tomb, and then, sharing her grief, I follow her with St. John and the holy women.

II. In returning to Jerusalem, they had to pass by the Cross, and St. Bonaventure tells us that "when they came again to it, our Blessed Lady knelt down and adored, saying: Here died, my dear, my precious Son; here He poured out the generous sea of blood for man's redemption: and after her example, all did the same. Nor is it without good grounds that we may believe our Blessed Lady to have been the first reverer of the Cross." O my dearest Mother, teach me also how to adore the Cross of thy Divine Son. Thou wert the first to follow Him on His painful course, the first, too, by staying at each of the stations, to commence the devotion of the Way of the Cross, which the Church has so richly indulgenced. I will follow thee too, O Mary, while thy sufferings call forth my compassion.

"When they drew nigh to the city, the women veiled her like a widow, and walked distressful and afflicted before her, and she proceeded after them with her head and face quite covered, between St. John and St. Mary Magdalen." It is thus that St. Bonaventure describes their return to Jerusalem.

*Resolution.* I will always venerate with the greatest respect the relics of the true Cross, whenever they are exposed in the Churches, either on feasts of the Holy Cross, or during Lent.

*Prayer.* O Mary, make me understand and share the sufferings of thy heart.

## CHAPTER CVI.

### THE AGONISING HEART OF MARY.

Thy own soul a sword shall pierce.
. . . . . . . . .
And his mother kept all these words in her heart.—*St. Luke* ii. *35, 51.*

> Oh, how sad and sore distressed
> Was that Mother highly blest
> Of the sole-begotten One!
> . . . . .
> Virgin of all virgins best!
> Listen to my fond request:
> Let me share thy grief divine.
> —*Stabat Mater.*

*Preparatory Prayer.* O Lord, I offer Thee all my thoughts and desires; do Thou deign to bless them.

I. Our Blessed Lady returns to Jerusalem quite overcome by sorrow. The holy women remain with her all the long hours of Friday and Saturday, and try to tend her as best they can. My place also is by her side, and I, too, will do all in my power to show her how my heart shares the grief of hers. I behold St. Mary Magdalen and some of the other women preparing perfumes to take to the sepulchre early in the morning. Their loving eagerness is very comforting to Mary in and St. Mary Magdalen." It is thus that St. Bonaventure describes their return to Jerusalem.

*Resolution.* I will always venerate with the greatest respect the relics of the true Cross, whenever they are exposed in the Churches, either on feasts of the Holy Cross, or during Lent.

*Prayer.* O Mary, make me understand and share the sufferings of thy heart.

## CHAPTER CVI.

### THE AGONISING HEART OF MARY.

Thy own soul a sword shall pierce.
. . . . . . . . . .
And his mother kept all these words in her heart.—*St. Luke* ii. *35, 51.*

> Oh, how sad and sore distressed
> Was that Mother highly blest
> Of the sole-begotten One!
> . . . . .
> Virgin of all virgins best!
> Listen to my fond request:
> Let me share thy grief divine.
> —*Stabat Mater.*

*Preparatory Prayer.* O Lord, I offer Thee all my thoughts and desires; do Thou deign to bless them.

I. Our Blessed Lady returns to Jerusalem quite overcome by sorrow. The holy women remain with her all the long hours of Friday and Saturday, and try to tend her as best they can. My place also is by her side, and I, too, will do all in my power to show her how my heart shares the grief of hers. I behold St. Mary Magdalen and some of the other women preparing perfumes to take to the sepulchre early in the morning. Their loving eagerness is very comforting to Mary in her grief. Let me, then, consider if I cannot do more for our dear Lady than merely show my devotion by words or prayers. It is not sufficient to grieve and pray. Love for Jesus should show itself in acts. I will then, like Mary Magdalen and her companions, who prepare precious perfumes to offer at Jesus' tomb, prepare the perfume of virtue and sacrifice, by trying, from this very moment, to be obedient, meek and mortified, and faithfully to fulfil all my duties.

II. But whilst these holy women are thus actively engaged in preparing their spices, and placing them in vessels that they may themselves carry them to the place of sepulchre, outside the town, what is our Blessed Lady doing? She remains silent and recollected—the expression of her calm and beautiful countenance is one of the deepest sorrow; her face, all surrounded as it is by her veil, appears quite sweet and heavenly. How different is her grief, intense though it be, from that of the other holy women. They are weeping for Jesus, but in their sorrow they forget our Lord's promises. They think only of His death, without remembering that He is to rise again, and they believe that they have lost everything because He has left them. But St. Bonaventure tells us: "Our Blessed Lady remained with a peaceful and serene mind, being always firm and constant in the certain hopes of her Son's Resurrection; in which hopes she persisted the whole Sabbath, for which reason, the Sabbath is a day specially dedicated to her by the Church." O

Agonising Heart of Mary, that alone in the new-born Church didst that day preserve the faith, and, borne up by thy interior remembrance of Jesus' words, didst honour in advance His glorious Resurrection, obtain for me the grace of a firm faith in our Lord's promises.

*Resolution.* I will often ask God, by Mary's suffering heart, to restore the faith to the many indifferent people, that, alas! are now in the world.

*Prayer.* My God, re-enkindle the faith in Catholic countries, by the intercession of the Immaculate Heart of Mary.

## CHAPTER CVII.

### THE RESURRECTION.

He is not here, but is risen.—*St. Luke xxiv. 6.*
Jesus Christ appears first to His Blessed Mother after His Resurrection. The Gospel leads us to think so, by saying that Jesus Christ appeared to several persons.—*St. Ignatius.*

*Preparatory Prayer.* I consecrate all my thoughts to Thee, O my God; deign, I beg of Thee, to bless them.

I. Early in the morning, on the day after the Sabbath, Mary Magdalen, Mary the mother of St. James, and Salome leave the Blessed Virgin alone, in order to go to the sepulchre. Mary is still, as on the previous day, profoundly recollected, and awaiting her Son's Resurrection. It is now daybreak of the third day foretold by Him. Her faith sustains her, though her sufferings are very great. I shall perhaps better understand the feelings of her heart, if I think of the grief of those mothers whom I may have seen weeping for the loss of a child. What dreadful anguish rends their hearts! Still Mary prayed, and St. Bonaventure imagines her prayer to be as follows:—"Most merciful Father, full of clemency and pity, You know that my most beloved and blessed Son is now dead and buried, and that He was first cruelly fixed to a disgraceful Cross between two thieves, and that after He had resigned His Blessed Soul to You, I myself helped to place His Sacred Body in the sepulchre. But as it is in Thy power to restore Him again safely to me, I beseech Thy Divine Majesty to do it." She was thinking over in her heart Jesus' acts and His compassion for the afflicted, the raising to life of Lazarus, of the daughter of Jairus, and especially how He consoled the widow of Naim in giving her back her only son. The remembrance of the past strengthened her. In moments of anxiety I should act as Mary did, and remember on how many occasions our Lord has helped and sustained me by His paternal intervention.

II. St. Bonaventure represents Mary as thus praying to her absent Son:—"O my most sweet Jesus, where art Thou now? What art Thou doing, and why dost Thou stay so long before Thou comest to relieve me? Make no longer delay, I beseech Thee, but come: for Thou Thyself saidst that Thou wouldst rise the third day, and is not this the third day? Rise therefore, my Beloved, my Joy, and comfort me with Thy presence, whom Thou hast so much afflicted with Thy absence." And he tells us that "as our Lady was thus praying, and shedding floods of tears, our Blessed Lord appeared suddenly to her, and stood before her in white, and with pleasing and loving aspect, solaced her, saying: *Hail, holy Mother:* And she, surprised with sudden joy, said: *Art Thou my blessed Son Jesus?* And bowing down, she adored Him."

III. O Jesus, remember that once Thou didst allow me to approach Thy Crib, as a little beggar and poor slave, unworthy to appear before Thee; grant me now a like favour, and allow me, in my turn, once more to gaze upon Thee. Let me also contemplate Thy Mother, whose joy is unbounded in Thy presence. With what happiness she beholds Thee again! Thou art now all resplendent with light and grace, but the marks of the Sacred Wounds in Thy Hands and Feet make me remember that Thou didst die for me. Yes, Thou art still the same sweet Saviour: I will try to know Thee better, so as to love Thee more, and follow more closely in Thy footsteps. O Lord, Thy glorious Resurrection overwhelms me with joy; I wish never more to leave Thee, and I beg of Thee so to fill my soul with heavenly things, that I may be Thine now and for ever!

*Resolution.* I will always try to enter into the spirit of the Church, at the different feasts of the year: to share her joy at Christmas and Easter, her grief and penance during Lent and Passiontide.

*Prayer.* O glorious and risen Jesus, Who hast conquered death, abide always with me, and destroy whatever is contrary to Thy rule in my heart!

www.ingramcontent.com/pod-product-compliance
Lightning Source LLC
Chambersburg PA
CBHW022056230426
43672CB00008B/1191